The First Court House of Meigs County, built in Chester, in 1822. Chester Academy Built 1842.

THE

Pioneer History of Meigs County

THE

Pioneer History of Meigs County

BY

STILLMAN CARTER LARKIN

ISBN: 978-93-5128-853-4(HB)

First Published in 1908
Indian Reprint in 2017

Published by

Kalpaz Publications
C-30, Satyawati Nagar,
Delhi – 110052
E-mail: kalpaz@hotmail.com
Website: kalpazpublications.com
Ph.: +91-9212142040

Cataloging in Publication Data—DK
Courtesy: D.K. Agencies (P) Ltd. <docinfo@dkagencies.com>

Larkin, Stillman Carter, 1808-1891, **author.**
The pioneer history of Meigs County / by Stillman Carter Larkin.
pages cm
"First published in 1908"—Title page verso.
ISBN 9789351288534

1. Meigs County (Ohio)—History. 2. Meigs County (Ohio)—Biography. I. Title.

F497.M53L37 2017 DDC 977.199 23

STILLMAN C. LARKIN

INTRODUCTION

In 1876 a revival of interest in local history was manifest throughout the United States. The Centennial of the Nation—the Exposition at Philadelphia, exhibiting trophies of the Revolutionary period, while much attention was bestowed upon Colonial relics, and regard for Colonial ancestry. The older class of people had been retired from public observation, especially in the Western States of Ohio, Indiana, Illinois and Michigan. The first settlers—the earlier emigrants—had braved the Indians, the wild beasts, the privations of a new country, had toiled to open up the primeval forests for cultivation, and broken in health, dispirited often by adversity, they had grown old before their "three-score-years and ten," and the generation following them had been unwittingly pushing them aside. They were in the way of modern progress, and they had retreated to the back rooms of their children's mansions. But in 1876 it was seen that the country could not celebrate her Centenary without bringing into honorable recognition the fathers and mothers, the soldiers and statesmen, whose achievements had wrought such evident prosperity for the country—such high rank among the Nations. So it came about that old records, old furniture, old tales of early days, old people tottering on their canes, were subjects of especial attention.

The Revolutionary soldier, old and gray, was escorted to a seat on the platform where jubilant oratory proclaimed his deeds of heroism. It was at this time that Stillman C. Larkin, Aaron Stivers, H. B. Smith and a few others, awakened to the fact that Meigs county had a past worthy of record, and in looking around discovered that the founders, the early emigrants, were gone! Not a representative left of the days of St. Clair, of men who came into this part of the county before Ohio was admitted into the Union. They became impressed with a sense of duty toward those forefathers, and to retrieve as far as possible the neglect of previous years, they organized the Meigs County Pioneer Association—H. B. Smith, President; Aaron Stivers, Secretary; later Stillman C. Larkin, President. Mr. Larkin as a son of a pioneer, Abel Larkin, who had been active in the organization and development of the civil and moral interests of the new country, began collecting and placing in manuscript, everything available of the acts and actors of all legislative affairs in the new country. First, the sparsely settled lands were incorporated in Washington county, and Marietta people were wise enough to keep a running account with Time, but Gallia county was taken out from Washington, and until 1819 all civil records were kept in Gallipolis, when Meigs county was taken out from Gallia county.

Mr. Larkin began at the beginning, and wrote the Declaration of Independence, declared in 1776, which made the Centennial of 1876 possible—he wrote out the Ordinance of 1787, that proclaimed freedom of the whole Northwest Territory of the Ohio river, from involuntary servitude of man for man. The first emigrants to Ohio—Washington, Gallia and Meigs, opened up the wilderness for cultivation, or the present generation would not have broad acres in meadows, or hillsides in wheat, or blooming fruit-laden orchards. These first settlers built their cabins and schoolhouses, had teachers for their children; they organized townships, elected township officers and kept records of local affairs.

For these men and these records Mr. Larkin had respect. It was no easy matter to collect and place in order the history of the first ten years of the settlements included later in the boundaries of Meigs county; for from 1798 to 1808, is an almost forgotten page, but the men who wrought for the good of coming generations—wrought wisely, intelligently, with broad views, and persistent effort to establish homes, roads, schools and churches, to assist in framing wholesome laws, and enforcing them for the protection and well-being of a growing community, men like George W. Putnam, Fuller Elliott, Levi Stedman, Brewster Higley, Peter Grow, Hamilton Kerr, John Miles, William Parker, Abel Larkin and others, whose deeds and names belong to the annals of those years from 1792 to 1808. That makes true pioneer history. From 1808 to 1818 the influx of emigrants increased rapidly. People seeking lands to found homes for their families, mechanics of all kinds, carpenters, blacksmiths, tanners and shoemakers, served for public utility and improvement.

In 1819 Meigs county was set off from Gallia county, and assumed importance. A court house and jail were built in Chester, the county seat. Courts of Common Pleas were held judges were appointed, county officers were elected—auditor, treasurer, recorder, sheriff and clerk of the courts. Township officers were chosen—esquires and constables, clerk, treasurer, assessor, trustees, school directors and supervisors. The discomforts of pioneer life had ceased. The people enjoyed comfortable homes, with growing families. From 1820 to 1830, there was an inflow of newcomers, representing all pursuits, civil and educational, lawyers, doctors, preachers and teachers. Farms changed owners, and new customs were introduced. The fertile Letart bottoms sent flatboats laden with produce annually on trips to the South, New Orleans being the final mart. The traders returning by keelboat or steamboat brought sugar and molasses, rice and coffee for the merchants and communities.

Nial Nye, Sr., & Sons were established at the mouth of Kerr's run, before the county of Meigs was organized, and kept a store of general merchandise, ran a sawmill, and had a boat landing, "a port of entry" for goods consigned to Levi Stedman and others at Chester and the interior of the county. A postoffice was located here and the place was called Nyesville. From 1820 to 1830, while a growing prosperity was seen throughout the county, no capitalist with means and energy had arrived to develop the natural resources of Meigs county. From 1830 to 1840 marked the beginning of commercial prosperity. Mr. V. B. Horton, with a wide personal influence, brought capital to operate on the development of the coal in the hills of Salisbury. He started the transportation of coal by means of a steamboat, the Condor, towing immense fleets laden with coal down the Ohio river, and farther down the Mississippi to the Gulf of Mexico, from whence ships conveyed it to Boston, and grates in Boston parlors glowed with Pomeroy coal. This enterprise opened up boat building—ship builders from Maine and Nova Scotia came to work and direct the labor in the Horton boat yard. It gave employment to river men to manage the tow-boat Condor, and the barges. English and Welch men of experience and judgment took charge of the mines, and miners from England, Wales and Germany went into the coal tunnels of Meigs county and with pick and hand-car brought to light the wealth of the hills. A rolling mill was set in operation, a foundry, machine shop, and Haven & Stackpole erected a three-story steam flouring mill. Pomeroy was laid out, lots sold, the town incorporated, and elegant residences were placed on the spurs of the hills at Naylor's run and Sugar run, while under the cliffs the Brothers Howe, Dr. Estes and the lawyer, U. G. Howe, Charles Pomeroy and Horace Horton built no less fine homes. Mr. Samuel Grant's sawmill had full orders, furnishing lumber as fast as possible. In this decade of stirring material prosperity, the little postoffice town of Graham's Station received an impetus. Mr. Lucius Cross came from Marietta in 1822 to lands of his own, and started a tannery, built flat boats to send hay to the South, opened a store of general merchandise, erected a mill on Bowman's run for making flour, and sawing lumber, giving employment to hundreds of men in these different enterprises. The name of Graham Station was changed to Racine. The town of Sheffield sprang into existence in these times, broad acres just above the mouth of Leading creek were laid out in lots, the town incorporated and a cotton mill built by Mr. Philip Jones, a novel project for a non-cotton producing territory. The Grant brothers put into the business of steam a flouring mill that prospered for more than forty years. The one great event in Meigs county was the removal of the county seat from Chester and establishing the seat of justice in Pomeroy.

The aim and intent of Mr. Larkin's book is to preserve a record of pioneer times, that later generations may have proper respect and pride in their forefathers. He was the prime mover in organizing the "Meigs County Pioneer Association," and devoted time, thought and research in order to place correct statements concerning those early days in his book.

We ask the "Pioneer Association of Meigs County" for a liberal patronage of the book, and of thinking men and women, who will find much to interest them in reading the work, and especially the favor of descendants of early settlers in Meigs county, who are scattered in other states and terrtories.

EMELINE LARKIN BICKNELL,
Reviser of the MSS. of S. C. Larkin.

THE DECLARATION OF INDEPENDENCE, JULY FOURTH, SEVENTEEN HUNDRED AND SEVENTY-SIX.

When in the course of human events it becomes necessary for one people to dissolve the political bands which have connected them with another, and to assume among the powers of earth, the separate and equal station to which the laws of nature and of Nature's God entitle them, a decent respect to the opinions of mankind requires that they should declare the causes which compel them to a separation.

We hold these truths to be self-evident that all men are created equal, that they are endowed by their Creator with certain inalienable rights; that among these are life, liberty and the pursuit of happiness. That to secure these rights, governments are instituted among men, deriving their just powers from the consent of the governed, and that whenever any form of government becomes destructive of these ends, it is the right of the people to alter or abolish it, and to institute new government, laying its foundations on such principles and organizing its powers in such form, as to them shall seem most likely to effect their safety and happiness.

Prudence indeed, will dictate that governments long established should not be changed for light and transient causes, and accordingly all experience hath shown that mankind are more disposed to suffer while evils are sufferable, than to right themselves by abolishing the form to which they are accustomed.

But when a long train of abuses and usurpations pursuing invariably the same object, evinces a design to reduce them under absolute despotism, it is their right, it is their duty to throw off such government, and provide new guards for their future security.

Such has been the patient sufferance of the colonies, and such is now the necessity which constrains them to alter their former system of government.

The history of the present king of Great Britain is a history of repeated injuries and usurpations, all having in direct object the establishment of an absolute tyranny over these states.

To prove this let these facts be submitted to a candid world: He has refused his assent to pass laws the most wholesome and necessary for the public good. He has forbidden his governors to pass laws of immediate and pressing importance, unless suspended in their operation till his assent should be obtained, and when so suspended, he has utterly neglected to attend to them. He has refused to pass other laws for the accommodation of large districts of people unless those people would relinquish their right of representation in the legislature, a right inestimable to them and formidable to tyrants only. He has called together legislative bodies at pleasure, unusual and uncomfortable and distant from the repository of their public records, for the sole purpose of fatiguing them into compliance with his measures. He has dissolved representative houses repeatedly for opposing with manly firmness his invasions on the rights of the people. He has refused for a long time after such dissolutions, to cause others to be elected whereby the legislative powers incapable of annihilation have returned to the people for their exercise. The States remaining in the meantime exposed to all the dangers of invasion from without, and convulsions within. He has endeavored to prevent the population of these states, for that purpose obstructing the laws for naturalization of foreigners, refusing to pass others to encourage their migration hither, and raising the conditions of new appropriations of lands. He has obstructed the administration of justice by refusing his assent to laws for establishing judiciary powers. He has made judges dependent on his will alone for the tenure of their offices and the amount and payment of their salaries. He has erected a multitude of new offices and sent hither swarms of officers to harass our people and eat out their substance. He kept among us in times of peace a standing army without the consent of our legislators. He has affected to render the military independent of and superior to the civil power. He has combined with others to subject us to a jurisdiction foreign to our Constitution and unacknowledged by our laws, giving his assent to their acts of pretended legislation.

For quartering large bodies of armed troops among us; for potecting them by a mock trial and punishment for any murders which they should commit on the inhabitants of these states; for cutting off our trade with all parts of the world; for imposing taxes on us without our consent; for depriving us in many cases of the benefits of trial by jury; for transporting us beyond seas to be tried for pretended offenses; for abolishing the free system of English laws in a neighboring province, establishing therein an arbitrary government and enlarging its boundaries, so as to render it at once an example and fit instrument for introducing the same absolute rule into these colonies; For taking away our charter, abolishing our most valuable laws and altering fundamentally the forms of our government; for suspending our own legislatures and declaring themselves invested with power to legislate for us in all cases whatsoever. He has abdicated government here by declaring us out of his protection and waging war against us.

He has plundered our seas, ravaged our coasts, burned our towns and destroyed the lives of our people. He is at this time transporting large armies of foreign mercenaries to complete the work of death, desolation and tyranny already begun with circumstances of cruelty and perfidy scarcely paralleled in the most barbarous ages, and totally unworthy the head of a Christian nation. He has constrained our fellow citizens, taken captive on the high seas to bear arms against their country, to become the executioners of their friends and brethren, or to fall themselves by their hands.

He has excited domestic insurrection among us and has endeavored to bring the inhabitants of our frontiers under the merciless Indian savages, whose known rule of warfare is an undistinguished destruction of all ages, sexes and conditions. In every stage of these oppressions we have petitioned for redress in the most humble terms. Our repeated petitions have been answered only by repeated injury. A prince whose character is thus marked by every act which may define a tyrant is unfit to be the ruler of a free people.

Nor have we been wanting in attentions to our British brethren. We have warned them from time to time of the attempts by their legislature to extend an unwarrantable jurisdiction over us. We have reminded them of the circumstances of our emigration and settlement here. We have appealed to their native justice and magnanimity and we have conjured them by the ties of our common kindred to disavow these usurpations which would inevitably interrupt our connections and correspondence. They, too, have been deaf to the voice of justice and consanguinity. We must, therefore, acquiesce in the necessity which denounces our separation; and hold them as we hold the rest of mankind, enemies in war; in peace, friends. We, therefore, representatives of the United States of America, in general Congress assembled, appealing to the Supreme Judge of the world for the rectitude of our intentions, do in the name and by the authority of the good people of these Colonies, solemnly publish and declare that these United Colonies are, and of right ought to be, free and independent states.

That they are absolved from all allegiance to the British crown, and that all poltical connection between them and the state of Great Britain is and ought to be totally dissolved; and that as free and independent states they have full power to levy war, conclude peace, contract alliances, establish commerce and to do all other acts and things which an independent state may of right do.

And for the support of this declaration with a firm reliance on the protection of Divine Providence, we mutually pledge to each other our lives, our fortunes and our sacred honor, July fourth, seventeen hundred and seventy-six. John Hancock, President.

Signers Names.

Georgia—Button Gwinnett, Lyman Hall, George Walton.

New Hampshire—Josiah Bartlett, William Whipple, Matthew Thornton.

Massachusetts Bay—Samuel Adams, John Adams, Robert Treat Paine, Elbridge Gerry.

Rhode Island—Stephen Hopkins, William Ellery.

Connecticut—Roger Sherman, Samuel Huntington, William Williams, Oliver Wolcott.

New York—William Floyd, Philip Livingstone, Francis Lewis, Lewis Morris.

New Jersey—Richard Stockton, John Witherspoon, Francis Hopkinson, Abraham Clark and John Hart.

Pennsylvania—Robert Morris, Benjamin Rush, Benjamin Franklin, John Morton, George Clymer, James Smith, John Hancock, George Taylor, James Wilson, George Ross.

Delaware—Caesar Rodney, George Read, Thomas McKean.

Maryland—Samuel Chase, William Paca, Thomas Stone, Charles Carroll, of Carrollton.

Virginia—George Wythe, Richard Henry Lee, Thomas Jefferson, Benjamin Harrison, Thomas Nelson, Jr., Francis Lightfoot Lee, Carter Braxton.

North Carolina—William Hooper, Joseph Hewes, John Penn.

South Carolina—Edward Rutledge, Thomas Hayward, Thomas Lynch, Arthur Middleton.

THE ORDINANCE OF 1787.

[Extract from the History of the United States of America, by Timothy Pitkin, Vol. 2, Page 214.]

In consequence of cessions the United States became possessed of all the lands northwest of the Ohio, and the establishment of a government for the inhabitants already settled, as well as others who might remove these, became necessary.

(The Colonial Congress, then in session at New York.)

This Congress, therefore, in July, 1787, established an Ordinance for the government of this territory.

This Ordinance is the basis of the governments established by Congress in all the territories of the United States, and may be considered an anomaly in American legislation. The whole territory was under one district, subject to be divided into two, at the pleasure of Congress.

With respect to the mode of governing the settlers in this territory or colony, the ordinance provided that until the number of free male inhabitants of full age in the district should amount to five thousand, the legislative, executive and judicial power should be vested in a governor and three judges, who, together with a secretary, were to be appointed by Congress. The governor was to remain in office three years and the judges during good behavior. The governor, with the judges were empowered to adopt and publish such laws of the original states, criminal and civil, as might be necessary, and best suited to the circumstances of the district, and report them to Congress; such laws to be in force until disapproved by that body. The governor was empowered to divide the district into counties or townships and to appoint all civil officers. As soon as the free, male inhabitants of full age and should amount to five thousand, a general assembly was to be constituted, to consist of the governor, a legislative council, and house of representatives. The representatives to be chosen from the counties or townships, one for every five hundred free, white male inhabitants, until the number should amount to twenty-five, after that the number to be regulated by the legislature. A representative must have been a citizen of the United States for three years, and be a resident of the district, or have resided three years in the district, in either case to have the fee simple of two hundred acres of land in the district. An elector was to reside in the district, have a freehold of fifty acres of land therein, and be a citizen of one of the states, or a like freehold and two years residence. The representatives to be chosen for two years.

The legislative council was to consist of five persons, to continue five years in office, unless sooner removed by Congress, were chosen in the following manner: The house of representatives to nominate ten persons, each possessed of a freehold in five hundred acres of land; out of this number Congress was to appoint five to constitute the council. The general assembly had power to make laws for the government of the district not repugnant to the Ordinance. All laws to have the sanction of the majority of both houses, and the assent of the governor. The legislative assembly were authorized by joint ballot to elect a delegate, who was to have a seat in Congress with the right of debating, but not of voting.

It was necessary to establish certain principles as the basis of the laws, constitutions, and governments, which might be formed in the territory, as well as to provide for its future political connection with the American confederacy. Congress, therefore, at the same time established certain articles, which were to be considered as articles of compact between the original states and the people of the territory, and which were to remain unalterable unless by common consent. By these no person in the territory was ever to be molested on account of his mode of worship, or religious sentiments, and every person was entitled to the benefits of the writ of habeas corpus, trial by jury, and all those other fundamental rights usually inserted in American bills of rights. Schools, and the means of education were forever to be encouraged, and the utmost good faith to be observed toward the Indians; particularly their lands and property were never to be taken from them without their consent.

The territory and the states to be formed therein were forever to remain a part of the American confederacy, but not less than three, nor more than five states, were to be established.

The bounds of these were fixed with liberty for Congress to alter them, by forming one or two new states in that part of the territory lying north of an east and west line drawn through the southern bend, or extreme of Lake Michigan. It was also provided that whenever in any of these states there should be sixty thousand free inhabitants, such state was to be admitted into the Union, on the same terms or footing of the original states in all respects whatever, and be at liberty to form a permanent constitution and government, such constitution and government was to be republican and conform to the principles of the articles.

If consistent with the general interests of the confederacy such state, however, might be admitted into the Union with a less number than sixty thousand free inhabitants. By the sixth and last article it was provided there should be neither slavery nor involuntary servitude in the territory otherwise than in the punishment of crime, of which the party should have been duly convicted, and in consequence of this lastwise and salutary provision the evil of slavery has been prevented in all the new states formed out of this territory northwest of the river Ohio."

NOTE.—Mr. Dana of Massachusetts is said to be the author of the sixth article.

P. S.—When this ordinance was being framed in New York City, the Constitutional Convention was preparing a Constitution for the Nation in Philadelphia.

THE OHIO LAND COMPANY'S PURCHASE.

The Ohio Land Company originated with the disbanded officers of the Revolutionary army, while a large portion of the stockholders were citizens at large. This company was organized in Boston early in the year 1787. The purchase from Congress consisted of a million and a half acres of land by negotiations made by Rev. Manassah Cutler, in 1787. The State of Ohio was admitted into the Union in 1802, and comprised that portion of the Northwest Territory on its eastern boundary, extending from the Ohio river on the south to the shores of Lake Erie on the north, comprising seventeen million five hundred thousand acres of very fine land. The lands of the Ohio Company's purchase were located in the southern part of the state bordering on the Ohio river.

These lands were surveyed by men appointed by the President, George Washington, of whom were General Tupper, General Meigs, General Israel Putnam, Colonel Ebenezer Sproat, John Matthews, and others. These surveyors divided the lands into townships containing six square miles, and these townships were sub-divided into ranges, and further surveyed into sections of 640 acres. Townships, ranges, and sections were numbered, as were 100-acre lots, which sold to purchasers. In every township, three sections are reserved for Congress, Ministerial and school purposes. The boundaries of these lands were permanent, thus, when any county or township or road refers to certain points—Township 2, Range 11, Section 6—it has reference to the surveys of the Ohio Company's purchase.

Meigs County.

Meigs county was formed in June, 1819, and was composed of territory set off from Gallia county, Athens county, and Washington county, and contained the following townships:

From Gallia County.—Letart township, organized in 1803; Salisbury township, organized in 1805; Rutland township, organized in 1812; Lebanon township, organized in 1813; Salem township, organized in 1814; Sutton township, organized 1814.

From Athens County.—Orange township, set off in 1813; Olive township, set off in 1819; Scipio township, set off in 1819; Columbia township, set off in 1820; Bedford, including Chester, township, set off in 1821.

NAMES OF HEADS OF FAMILIES IN LEBANON, LETART, AND SUTTON TOWNSHIPS, OHIO, 1820.

Lebanon Township.

Caleb Price
David Pickens
Simeon Lawrence
George Warth
George Commins
William Pickens
John Flesher
Jacob Regor
James Giles
Lucinda Flesher
John Hall
Thomas Flinn
John Smith
Charles Shipman
Abraham Knapp
Ziba Lindley, Jr.
Edward Anderson
Ziba Lindley
Stephen K. Miller
Andrew Anderson
John Sissle
Thomas Lloyd
Robert Pickens
David Dailey
Jacob Buffington
Aaron Lasley
William Smith
William Barringer
Elias Browning
Joseph Buffington
David Sleath
Edward Sims
Lawrence Jenks
John Brown
Samuel M. Jackson
Hugh Brown
Catharine Alford
Philip Lauck
William Lauck
Levi T. Gandy
John Hanshaw
Solomon Smith

Letart Township.

John H. Sayre
Samuel A. Deviney
Benjamin Warner
Isaac Taylor
Baltzer Roush
Adam Harpold
Michael Roush
Henry Roush, Jr.

Molly Roller
David Wheelbarger
Elizabeth Wolf
Thomas Vail
John Linscott
Michael Darst
Peter Wolf
George Hrell
Anthony Roush
Henry Roush
Edward McDade
Ephraim Sayre
David C. Sayre
John Waggoner
Ezra Chapman
George Burns
David B. Sayre
John Sayre
Job Powell
Burton Bradford
John Hayman
James Hayman
John S. White
William Alexander
John Boudinot
Thomas Love
Moses Sayre
Lydia Slack
Reubin Smith
Levi Osborn
Moses Goodfellow
Peter R. Goodfellow
John McElroy
Samuel Clark
Niece Pickens
Milby German
Jacob Scott
John Deviney
Thomas Sayre
Elizabeth Deviney
William Smith
Calvin Martin
Jacob Crowser
Robert Sayre
Spencer Hayman
Jedediah Darby
Theopholus Ketchan
Elijah Bebee
Joseph Bebee
Abraham Kingree
William A. Boyce
Jonathan Evens
Robert Hester
Shadrack Rice
John Smith
Haviland Chase
Daniel Lovett
John Smith

Sutton Township.

John Pickens
George Ingals
Joseph Ingals
Aaron Thompson
Peter Wolf
William Kerr
Thomas Batey
John H. Hayman
Samuel Pickens
Jacob Wolf
Thomas Ashworth
James Ashworth
Isaac Foster
David Ashworth
Jacob Salser
Stephen Partlow
Robert Baird
Loftus Pullins
John Pullins
Michael Will
George Schibelair
John Ralph

Aaron Torrence
Simeon Elliott
Randall Stivers
James Pickens
Erastus Gelson
James McCormick
Cornelius Roush
Frances Hughs
John Hussey
William Radford
Jasper Branch
Wyman Hardy
Ezra Bemass
John R. Smith
Thompson Pickens
Jacob Aumiller
David Young
Asa Johnston
Benjamin Noyes
Jonathan Seelye
Edward Ward
George Roush
Mary White
Henry Wolf
Lyman Parker
Seth Jones
Fuller Elliott
Thomas Reding
John Wolf
Peter Lallance
George Wolf
Michael Circle
Sylvanus Ripley
Andrew Donley
John Quickle
Luther Donilson
Gabriel Walling
John Rose
John Frank
Thomas Smith
David Hudson
Anson Sole
Joel Hull
Stephen Root
Samuel Grant
David Curtis
David Cooper
Peter Masten
William Kimes
Solomon Wolf
Thomas Wigger
Samuel Westfall
Sarah Gilmore
William Watkins
Jacob McBride
Philip Watkins
James Blairs
Nathaniel Prentice
Lewis Chase
Richard Haden
Royal Burch
Michael Nease
Mary Burrell
Rogger McBride
Mary Dunbar
Adam Houdeshell
James Dixon
Michael Peltz
Philemon Warner
John Warner
Robert C. Barton
Nicholas Weaver
Charlotte Scott
Fenn Robinson
Hezekiah Sims
David Stewart
Jeremiah Shumway

Township boundaries were made anew, or within the limits of the older townships. Letart township originally extended from the mouth of Shade river to the mouth of Kerr's run and out of its territory the townships of Lebanon and Sutton were formed.

Salisbury township originally embraced territory as far north as Ross county, but such portions of the township as were within the boundaries of Meigs county were divided into Rutland township, Salem township, and a township remaining Salisbury. Deeds of land are recorded according to the nomenclature of the Ohio Company's surveys.

Ohio, having been admitted into the Union in 1802, it followed that a constitutional convention should be called to prepare a constitution for the new state, therefore, electors, or delegates, were elected according to the regulations given by the Congress of the United States, and according to the Ordinance of 1787, for the Northwest Territory, eliminating only one claim of that ordinance, viz: the property qualifications from the counties within its boundaries.

The Constitutional Convention was composed of thirty-five members. Washington county was entitled to four delegates, as follows: Rufus Putnam, Ephraim Cutler, Benjamin Ives Gilman, and John McIntyre. This convention assembled at Chillicothe, November 1st, 1802, and adjourned November 29th, 1802. That assembly formed Gallia county by a law that was to come in force April 30th, 1803, by a division of Washington county, with specified boundaries, but it was bounded on the west by Scioto county until 1816. Athens county was formed March 1st, 1805, and was bounded on the south by Gallia county until January 7th, 1807. The boundary of the south of Athens county was changed to take a portion on which Chester is located, from Gallia, and add it to Athens county, where it remained until the formation of Meigs county, April 1st, 1819.

An act of legislature authorizing associate judges to divide the counties into townships was made May 10th, 1803. In accordance therewith Gallia county was divided into three townships—Gallipolis, Kerr's, and Letart.

The same act of the legislature authorized the associate judges to appoint justices of the peace for each of the aforesaid townships. Robert Safford and George W. Putnam were appointed for Gallipolis township. In Letart township an election of justice of the peace was to be held in the house of Henry Roush—one justice of the peace for Letart township. For Kerr's township one justice of the peace was to be elected, and the election to be held in the house of William Robinson. Another act of the legislature creating a board of county commissioners came into force March 1st, 1804. The commissioners aforesaid on the 11th of June, 1805, proceeded to redivide the county of Gallia into townships, recognizing the boundaries of Letart, but abolishing that of Kerr's, and forming a new township by the name of Salisbury and establishing its boundaries as follows: Beginning on the Ohio river in the Thirteenth range of townships at the southeast corner of 100-acre lot No. 376; thence west with the south line of said lot to the southwest corner of the same; thence north to the southeast corner of Section No. 10, in Range No. 14, of Township No. 5; thence west to the line between the Fourteenth and Fifteenth ranges; thence north to the northwest corner of Township No. 5, in the Fourteenth range; thence west to the county line; thence north to the northwest corner of the county; thence east until it intersects the line between Kerr's and Letart; thence with the same to the Ohio river; thence down to the place of beginning.

The first election for township officers for Salisbury township was held in the house of Brewster Higley, Esq., July 27th, 1805.

Trustees Elected.—Hamilton Kerr, James G. Phelps, Felix Benedict.

Overseers of the Poor.—John Niswonger, William Parker.

Fence Viewers.—Samuel Denny, David Thomas.

Appraisers of Houses and Listers.—William Parker, Jr., Benjamin Smith.

Supervisors of Highways.—William Green, Abijah Hubbell, John Niswonger.

Constables.—James Smith, Jared Strong.

Treasurer.—Joel Higley, Jr.

Clerk.—Abel Larkin.

In accordance with the above order, John Niswonger and Horatio Strong were elected justices of the peace for Salisbury township, July 27th, 1805.

The names of the first settlers in territory included in Meigs county and the dates of their arrival, as follows:

James Smith, from Marietta, 1797; Levi Chapman, 1787; Thomas L. Halsey, 1792; Hamilton Kerr, 1797; Nicholas Brown, 1796; Joseph Russell, 1792; James Smith, 1797; William Russell, 1792; Brewster Higley, 1799; John Case, a surveyor, 1799; Levi Stedman, 1798; Peter Grow, 1798; Peter Shaw, 1792; Ezra Chapman, 1799; Shubael Burris, 1796; William Bradford, 1792; William Browning, 1795; Joshua Chapman, 1799; William Barton, 1792; George Warth, 1798; Peter Lalance, 1798; Fuller Elliot, agent for O. L. C. P., 1792; Livingston Smith, 1800; Josiah Rice, 1800; Samuel Denny, 1800; Thomas Everton, 1800; Jeremiah Riggs, 1800; Leonard Hedrick, 1800; George Ackley, 1800; Thomas Rairdon, 1800; William Coleman, 1800; John Miles, 1801; Captain James Merrill, 1801; Timothy Dexter, 1801; William Parker, Sr., 1802; Thomas Shepherd, 1802; Alshire Brothers, Conrad, Michael, and Peter, 1802; Joel Higley, 1803; Daniel Rathburn, 1803; Jabez Benedict, 1803; William Johnson; James E. Phelps, 1803; Caleb Gardner, 1803; Thomas Alexander, 1803; Elias Hall, 1803; William Buffington; Abel Larkin, 1804; Truman Hecox, 1804; Alvin Ogden, 1804; Shubael Nobles, 1804; Rev. Eli Stedman, 1804; Samuel Branch, 1804; Timothy Smith, 1805; Frederic Hysell, 1805; —— Bing, 1805; Luke Brine, 1805; Fuller Elliott, located in 1805; Jacob Wolf, 1805; Jeremiah Fogg, 1806; Aaron Holt, 1807; James and John Forrest, 1807; Thomas Gaston, 1807; Joel Cowdery, 1807; Henry Roush, 1808; Jacob Cowdery, 1808; Squire Bullock, 1808; Philip Buffington, 1808; Aaron Torrence, 1809; John Eutsminger, 1787; Josiah and Joseph Vining, 1810; Alexander Warth, 1810; John Hall, 1811; Richard Cook, 1811; Seth Jones, 1812; Adam Harpold, 1812; Augustine Webster, 1812; William Skinner, 1810; Samuel Everett, son-in-law of Ham. Kerr, 1812; John, Erastus, and Nathaniel Williams, 1812; Joseph Townsend, 1812; Dr. Philip Lauck, 1813; Andrew Anderson, 1814; Jedediah Darby, 1814; John Hayman, 1810; Peter Pilchard, 1810.

The electors for Governor of Ohio, 1805, in Salisbury township, were the following:

John Hilverson, James E. Phelps, John Niswonger, Elam Higley, William Sparks, Brewster Higley, Daniel Strong, Caleb Gardner, Cornelius Thomas, John Miles, William Green, Nimrod Hysell, Stephen Strong, Jared Strong, William Barker, Daniel Rathburn, Samuel Denny, Hamilton Kerr, Thomas Shephard, Benjamin Williams, Horatio Strong, Joel Higley, 1st, James Smith, William Spencer, Joel Higley, Jr., Abel Larkin, Samuel Ervin, Felix Benedict.

The state elections for Governors and state officers were held on the second Tuesday in October, 1802, and until November, 1886, when, by a constitutional provision, the time was altered to conform to the time of holding elections for the Presidents of the United States.

Three road districts were made in Salisbury township in 1806 and the following supervisors elected, namely:

First District: Benjamin Smith, supervisor. He made returns for work done in 1806 to the trustees in 1807.

Second District: Daniel Rathburn, supervisor. He made returns for work done in 1806 to the trustees in 1807.

Third District: John Miles, supervisor. Returns made in 1807 for work done in 1806. The work on the highways was to pay a road tax. By a law of 1804 every male person over 18 years of age and under 50 years of age was liable yearly and every year to do three days work on the public roads. The trustees of Salisbury township levied a tax to be worked out at sixty-two and one-half cents a day.

Rutland township was organized in 1812, being formed out of territory embraced by Salisbury township, Gallia county, and consisted of Township 6, Range 14, of the Ohio Company's purchase. This Township 6 was divided by the original land company into thirty-six square miles, or sections of 640 acres each, commencing to number them at the southeast corner, running north. Three sections were secured to Congress, namely: Nos. 8, 11, and 26. For ministerial purposes No. 29, and for school purposes No. 16, making in all five sections. Nine sections near the center of the township were cut up into fractions of 262 acres each, as follows: Nos. 9, 10, 14, 15, 20, 21, 22, 27, 28. leaving twenty-two whole sections and twenty-two fractions for the company. The fractions in Rutland township are numbered so as to correspond with the sections belonging to the company, Nos. 1, 2, 3, 4, 5, 6, 7, 12, 13, 17, 18, 19, 23, 24, 25, 30, 31, 32, 33, 34, 35, 36. Six sections were added after the formation of Meigs county, April 1st, 1819, and are an important addition to Rutland township. Among the pioneers who settled on this tier of sections were Joel Higley, Jr., James E. Phelp, Daniel Rathburn, and Benjamin Williams, all from Granby, Connecticut, in 1803.

In looking back to the days when Salisbury township extended from Kerr's run westward to Ross county, we have introduced a list of some supervisors of roads, and after giving names, dates and returns, find it interesting to describe the boundaries of one or two road districts, viz, of Daniel Rathburn, Second district, ordered to do work, beginning at Widow Case's, down to the Butternut rock, when he thought most proper, this being highway tax for the year 1806:

Daniel Rathburn, $2.15; Joel Higley, $1.95; Brewster Higley, $2.65; Abel Larkin, $1.15; Luke Brine, 85 cents; Joel Higley, Jr., $1.45; James E. Phelps, $2.05; Shubael Nobles, $1.05; Esquire Bullock, $1.35; Eli Stedman, $1.15; Benjamin Williams, 75 cents; Elam Higley, 75 cents; Jesse Fleshman, $1.55; Jesse Carpenter, 85 cents; Edward Faller, $1.65; Moses Russell, $1.85; Martin Roup, $1.65; William Sparks, 95 cents; William Campbell, 85 cents; Nicholas Sins, $1.55; —— Stillwell, $1.55; Amos Carpenter, 75 cents.

JOEL HIGLEY,
JAMES E. PHELPS,
October 15th, 1806. Trustees.

John Miles, supervisor of the Third road district in Salisbury township, highway taxes for the year 1806, the district beginning at the Widow Case's, up the road to the 7-mile tree:

William Spencer, 95 cents; Abijah Hubbell, $1.35; John Miles, $1.55; Caleb Gardner, $1.65; Erastus Stow, $1.15; William Parker, Jr., $1.55; Thomas Shepherd, $1.35; Thomas Everton, 85 cents; Felix Benedict, $1.15.

WILLIAM PARKER,
JAMES E. PHELPS,
JOEL HIGLEY, JR.,
Trustees.

The Widow Case mentioned in the boundaries of the Second and Third road districts lived where the late lamented Virgil C. Smith afterwards lived. Mrs. Case was his maternal grandmother, who subsequently married Abijah Hubbel, Sr. She was the widow of John Case, mentioned, also, in the account of the settlement of Brewster Higley. Mr. Case had gone back to Vermont, and in company with his friend and neighbor, Noah Smith, started for Ohio. Mr. Case had a young wife, and Mr. Smith had a wife and three or four daughters, and son 3½ years old. After journeying on the road from Philadelphia as far as Carlisle, in Cumberland county, Noah

The Higley Homestead—One Hundred and Ten Years in the Family.

Smith suddenly died. His family went on with Mr. Case until reaching a little town West Liberty, the county seat of Ohio county, West Virginia, where John Case suddenly died, and where Mrs. Case gave birth to a daughter—her first child, who was named Eliza. As soon as these conditions were known by Brewster Higley he went to their relief and brought them all to Leading creek. Mrs. Smith settled on land bought of Samuel Denny, on the west side of the creek, and Mrs. Case settled on the east side of the same stream, and nearly opposite Mrs. Smith. There she brought up her daughter, Eliza, and the Smith family were reared, so in the later years Livingston Smith and Eliza Case were married, reared a respectable family, and died, after living to a good old age.

The Butternut rock is on the west side of Leading creek, half a mile above the mouth of Thomas fork. The 7-mile tree is thought to be on the road up Leading creek on the road traveled to Scioto salt furnaces, but the exact place is unknown—probably about Langsville.

BREWSTER HIGLEY AND FAMILY.

The first settlement made in Rutland township was by Brewster Higley, in April, 1799, on the farm since occupied by his son, Milo Higley. Judge Higley was a native of Simsbury, Connecticut, but came from Castleton, Rutland county, Vermont, to Bellville, West Virginia, where he remained 18 months, preparatory to his removal to Ohio. He bought a share in the Ohio Company's purchase for one thousand dollars. He then, in company with John Case, who had been one of a party of surveyors, and was of some service to Mr. Higley in making his selection of land, as he was to have a part of the land, made a visit to the place of his future home. He returned to Bellville, purchased a family boat and floated down the Ohio river to the mouth of Leading creek, which being high with back water, he poled his boat up the stream as far as the place known as Jacobs' upper salt works. Here he tore his boat to pieces and built a shanty for his family to live in until he could build a house on his land. The first shanty made for his boys and John Case to live in while clearing the land was made of bark and sticks and stood near the ground afterwards used as a family graveyard.

Brewster Higley was a Revolutionary soldier and had served as justice of the peace in the state of Vermont. General Arthur St. Clair, Governor of the Northwest Territory, appointed Brewster Higley as one of the justices of the peace for the county of Washington, the commission bearing date December 28th, 1801, done at Chillicothe. This commission and one to Fuller Elliot, of Letart, are probably the only ones for justices appointed under the territorial government for the people living in what is now Meigs county. Mr. Higley was one of the first associate judges of Gallia county and served for a number of years. He was elected justice of the peace in Rutland township, and in 1815 was made the second postmaster of Rutland and held the office for several years. He died June 20th, 1847, at the ripe old age of 88 years 3 months and 6 days. His wife, Naomi Higley, died February 4th, 1850, aged 89 years, one month and 3 days.

The children of Brewster Higley and his wife, Naomi Higley, were four sons and three daughters.

The sons were: Brewster Higley, Jr., who married Acksah Evarts.

Cyrus Higley married Electa Bingham, daughter of Judge Alvin Bingham, of Athens. One son, Julius Bicknell Higley.

Lucius Higley married Nancy Shepherd. Lucius Milton Higley married Miss Morton. Milo Higley married Miss Pankey.

Joseph L. Higley married Emily Reed.

Harriet Higley was married to Alvin Bingham, Jr., son of Judge Bingham, of Athens.

Theresa Higley was married to Josiah Simpson.

Susan Higley, the eldest child, never married, but lived with her parents until her decease.

In 1800 Samuel Denny came from Massachusetts and bought a tract of land, and built a cabin on it. This was near the Livingston Smith farm. He also helped to erect the first school house, and taught the first school in the winter 1801, also in 1802. The school consisted of nine scholars, four of whom came from near the mouth of Leading creek. The roll recorded the names of James Smith, John Smith, Sarah Kerr, Christina Niswonger, and five scholars from Judge Higley's family. In 1803 Samuel Denny built the first grist mill on Leading creek, which stood close to the residence of Jabez Hubbell. Mr. Denny delivered the first oration ever delivered here, at a Fourth of July celebration in 1806. The speaker stood on the top of an ancient mound not far from the Case house. Mr. Denny left Ohio in 1810, returned to Massachusetts, and married, and died there.

JOEL HIGLEY AND FAMILY.

In 1803 Joel Higley and his wife, Eunice Higley (nee Haskins) came from Granby, Connecticut (Lieutenant Higley he was called), and settled on the south tier of sections, in what was afterward included in Rutland township. There were twenty-eight persons in this company with Joel Higley.

Joel Higley, 1st, had a numerous and prolific family. The daughter, Rachel, married Williams, and remained in Connecticut. She was born in 1800.

Joel Higley, Jr., (called Major Higley) settled in the same neighborhood with his father. He was born July 31st, 1764, and married Cynthia Phelps, May 25th, 1785. She was a sister of James E. Phelps. Mr. Higley died April 26th, 1823, and his wife died January 5th, 1832.

Of this union there were three sons and five daughters. Polly Higley married Philip Jones in May, 1806. They lived on a farm where Middleport is now situated. Philip Jones died May 30th, 1866, aged 80 years.

Elihu Higley was born November 26th, 1788. He served in the Army of the Northwest in the War of 1812. He married Nancy Cook in December, 1815, moved to his farm in Rutland in December, 1816. They had one child, Clarissa Fidelia—married Martin Fox. Mr. Higley died April 23d, 1877, aged 89 years.

Laura Higley, born August 20th, 1795. She was married to Daniel C. Rathburn in 1812, in Rutland, O., moved to Indiana, died there in August, 1884, aged 91 years.

Sally Higley; born March 8th, 1795, was married to Daniel McNaughton, December, 1816, and died September 29th, 1845, aged 50 years. Harlow McNaughton, a son, was captain of the Seventh Ohio Battery in the Civil war for the Union.

Cynthia Higley, born February 7th, 1797, and never married. She died August 26th, 1819, aged 22 years.

Maria Higley, born July 30th, 1799, and married Willis Knight, and died February 28th, 1834, aged 35 years.

Joel Phelps Higley was born June 9th, 1802, married Catherine Wise, and died October 23d, 1836, aged 34. A son, Captain Joel P. Higley, fell in fighting for the Union in 1863.

Laurinda Higley was married to Earl P. Archer and died September, 1855, aged 90 years. She was the mother of a large family. Marinda Archer, Henry, Sophia, Benjamin, Elam, and Abiah Archer, who married Benjamin Whitlock, their children were Hiram, Electa, Levi, Harriet, Eunice.

Eunice Higley married Silas Knight, known as "Deacon Knight," in 1812 and came to Rutland in 1812. They were highly respected. They had a numerous family—two sons and six daughters. Mr. Knight and his wife, Eunice, both died the same day and were buried in the same grave, July 31st, 1839, aged 67 years and 63 years, respectively.

Electa Higley was born in 1778, and came to Rutland with her parents, and afterwards married Benjamin Williams. She

The Higley Family Grave-Yard.

was a remarkable woman, intelligent, energetic, with resourceful disposition to be adapted to pioneer conditions. She taught school in her own house, cut and made men's best clothes, and cared for a flower garden that was the pride of Rutland for many years. She had two children, a daughter, born February 21st, 1811, married Rev. James Mitchell, went to Illinois in 1855, and died February 3d, 1881. Mrs. Electa Williams died at her daughter's in Illinois, in 1865, aged 87 years. Her husband died July 26th, 1873. The son, Benjamin Selah Williams, was born November 18th, 1808, and married Elizabeth L. Brown, of Athens county, and lived on the homestead farm where he was born until his death, February 17th, 1891, aged 82 years, 3 months. Mrs. Williams was born July 2d, 1811, and died February 14th, 1897, aged 85 years, 7 months, 12 days. They had a numerous family of sons and daughters, but they, except two children, James and Mary, left Ohio for the West.

Sophia Higley was married to Asa Stearns, a Free Will Baptist preacher, finally settled in Mercer county, Ohio, where they both died. They had four children, Rufus, Amos, Louise, and Joel.

Elam Higley was a soldier in the War of 1812 and served under General Harrison in the Army of the Northwest. He married Sally Clarke, and settled on a farm in the northeast corner of Rutland township. They had one child, Austin Higley, who went to Iowa about 1876, and died there.

An incident in the life of Elam Higley is worth relating. After his enlistment, when about to leave home, his mother gave him a Bible with directions to put it in a side pocket of his coat, already made for its reception. When in the Maumee country they had a skirmish with the enemy, and a bullet fired by an Indian, aimed at Elam's heart, struck that Bible but did not pass through, thus his life was preserved. His comrades said, "Elam thought himself badly wounded, but the ball was found in the Bible, and he was not hurt."

Hamilton Kerr was born in Philadelphia in 1764. He was a noted Indian scout of great daring, courage and strength. He married Susannah Niswonger, a highly educated young woman, and daughter of Colonel John Niswonger. Mr. Kerr came to his land below the mouth of Leading creek, on the Ohio river, in 1797, and was an active, useful citizen, as seen in reports of all civil proceedings of Salisbury township. Of their children, William Kerr married Jane Murray and settled on a farm on the west side of Thomas fork, just above the mouth, where he died March 27th, 1883, aged 86 years.

Sarah Kerr was married to Samuel Everett, and lived near the mouth of Story's run; later moved to the northern part of Ohio.

Margaret Kerr was married to Hamilton Kerr, a distant relative.

After the death of Hamilton Kerr in 1821 the estate was settled by Colonel Everett, the administrator, and Mrs. Kerr, the widow, and her daughter, Sophia, moved to the north part of the state, probably Wyandot county.

Colonel John Niswonger was of German extraction and early in life was from near Winchester, Virginia. He enlisted December 29th, 1776, to serve during the war; served as a sergeant in Captain John Leman's company, Thirteenth Virginia regiment, commanded successively by Colonel John Gibson, Revolutionary war, and appears on the muster roll, October, November, and December, 1779, at Fort Pitt, and February 13th, 1780, on which he is reported as being at Fort Henry. Colonel John Niswonger was one of the heroes of the battle of Point Pleasant. He settled on land near the mouth of Leading creek, with his son-in-law, Hamilton Kerr, in 1798, and was an important factor in the civil arrangements for the government of Salisbury township, afterwards included in Rutland township, Meigs county. His tombstone was found in the tearing down of an old building, where it had been used as a hearthstone. It had this plain inscription: "Sacred to the memory of Colonel John Niswonger, who departed this life July 13th, 1821, aged 78 years and 4 months." No person now living can find the place of his grave.

Peter Niswonger was a comrade of George Warth in the hunting trips of the years 1811 to 1814, when Mr. Niswonger had a still-house for making whisky and peach brandy, built by a spring of excellent water, on Lot 182, Ohio Company's purchase, afterward owned by Nehemiah Bicknell. The spring was always called the "still-house spring." His name, in connection with that of Elias Nesselrode, is used in an account of an elk discovered crossing the Ohio river below Sandy creek, by Andrew Anderson, who, being on the Ohio side of the river, saw Niswonger and Nesselrode pushing a canoe laden with salt upstream to whom he called "to head off the elk," which had reached their side so near that they threw a log chain at his horns, which so enraged him that he capsized their canoe with the men and the salt and escaped to the woods of Virginia.

THE WARTH FAMILY—COLONEL DAVID BARBER'S LETTER, 1882.

"During the Indian war there came to the stockade in Marietta a family named George Warth, his wife and two daughters and five sons, namely: John, George, Robert, Martin, and Alexander. They came from Virginia, brought up in the woods and were all fine hunters. John and George were employed as rangers, or spies for Fort Harmar. The family lived in a log house on the first bottom between the river and the garrison built by the United States troops for the artificers to work in. George Warth married Ruth Fleehart, and John Warth married Sally Fleehart, sisters to Joshua Fleehart, and Robert Warth married a daughter of a French widow named Lallance, who came from France with two children, a son and this daughter, and who were in the stockade at the time when Robert Warth was killed by the Indians. He left a young widow and one child, Robert Warth, afterwards a noted merchant of Gallipolis. The family were illiterate, but possessed keen, clear intellectual faculties, which were improved in later years by whatever opportunities were afforded for learning.

Mr. Paul Fearing taught John Warth the rudiments of his education, which he cultivated so that at the close of Indian hostilities, having settled on lands in West Virginia, Jackson county, long known as Warth's bottom, he filled several offices for the government and was a magistrate for a number of years. He was also the owner of slaves. George Warth owned a piece of land in Meigs county, on the Ohio river, opposite the present town of Ravenswood, West Virginia. He, with his brother John, carried the first mails from Marietta to Gallipolis, in canoes. They went armed with rifles, carried provisions for their journey, traveling chiefly at night to avoid Indian encounters. George Warth was a hunter of wild animals, his greatest success during life. He had a family of sons and daughters—Robert Warth and Alexander Warth, Clara, Sally, Hannah, Rebecca, Rachel, and Drusilla. He lived and died in his cabin on the banks of the Ohio, a poor man in what the world calls wealth, yet all of the hero is due to his name, for brave and fearless protection of the helpless in times of peril.

The son, Robert Warth, married Mary Johnson, and lived as a farmer in Jackson county, West Virginia, and died in Ravenswood.

Alexander Warth was a boatman, married in Louisville, Kentucky, and after the death of his parents, within two weeks of each other, his sisters, Sally, Rachel, and Drusilla, moved to Louisville.

Rebecca Warth was married to Daniel Lovett, a river man, and they moved to Kentucky.

Hannah Warth was married to Bartholomew Fleming and lived and died in Ravenswood. Mr. Fleming bought the placed owned by Mr. George Warth, valued chiefly for the landing and ferrying opportunities.

Clara Warth was unmarried—died and is buried by the side of her mother in the Pioneer graveyard in Great Bend, Meigs county, Ohio."

FELIX BENEDICT, A PIONEER OF 1803 TO RUTLAND TOWNSHIP.

He was the son of Elisha Benedict, and his wife, Jerusha Starr Benedict, and was born May 13th, 1767. He, with his father, Elisha Benedict, were living at Cooperstown, New York, when in October, 1780, they were taken prisoners by the British and Indians, then taken to Canada where they were kept prisoners for two and a half years. He married Clarissa Hubbell, daughter of Jabez and Sarah Hubbell, of Otsego county, New York, and coming to Ohio, settled on a farm near where the village of Rutland is now. He was an active and influential citizen, prominent in every interest for the promotion of civil, educational or religious advancement for the moral good of the neighborhood in which he spent his long life. He died October 29th, 1828. Mrs. Benedict died July 9th, 1849. Their children:

Sarah, born October 25th, 1788, married John Dixon, died September 29th, 1835.

Polly, died young.

Euretta, born March 18th, 1793. She was married in 1821 to Cornelius Merrill. She died December 12th, 1880. They had six children, Mary, Robert, Luther, Harriet, Clarissa, and Augustus.

Elisha Hubbell Benedict, born September 15th, 1795. He married Maria Simpson, and they lived in Rutland township several years, but removed to Kansas in 1856, where Mrs. Benedict died. They had six children—Lydia Ann, Claretta, Sarah A., Elisha C., Walter. Elisha C. enlisted in Company D, Ninth Regiment, Kansas Volunteer Cavalry, and died at Fort Scott, Kansas, September 13th, 1862.

Walter F., born July 28th, 1845, enlisted in Company D, Ninth Kansas Regiment, Volunteer Infantry, served during the Civil war and participated in fifteen engagements.

Harriet, born December 15th, 1797, and married November 8th, 1829, to Benjamin Savage, and died November 9th, 1861.

Felix Starr, born May 3d, 1806, and died August 13th, 1824.

William Spencer, born November 28th, 1808, and died June 16th, 1833.

JABEZ BENEDICT AND FAMILY.

He was a son of Felix Benedict and wife, Clarissa, and was born October 13, 1802, and removed with his parents to Leading Creek, Ohio, October 13, 1803. He married April 4th, 1833, Miriam Chase, daughter of John and Miriam Chase, of Athens county, Ohio. Their children were four—Clarissa, born May 7th, 1835; William S., died young; John Merrill Benedict, born September 17th, 1839. He enlisted in the Eightenth Ohio Volunteer Infantry as a private and was promoted to lieutenant colonel, served four years in the Civil war, was wounded twice at Nashville, but recovered, and was brevetted colonel at the close of the war. He married October 18th, 1882, to Miss Bettie Rife, of Morgantown, West Virginia.

George W. Benedict, son of Jabez Benedict and wife, was born July 21st, 1843. He served three years in the Eighteenth Ohio Volunteer Infantry, was married March 4th, 1878, to Florence Grimes, a daughter of James Grimes, of Rutland, Ohio.

Jabez Benedict died January 28th, 1886. He was noted for his fondness for reading, and with a retentive memory he was familiar with the best authors of his time, and of the Holy Scriptures.

Thomas Everton came from Canada in 1800, and settled on a farm near the mouth of Leading creek. He was a member of the Regular Baptist Church and was called, familiarly, "Deacon Everton," and died on his farm in Rutland township. There were eight children: Betsy, Mrs. Benjamin Richardson; Ebenezer Everton; Relief, Mrs. Edwards; Thomas Everton, Jr.; Polly, Mrs. Stone; Nancy, Mrs. Jesse W. Stevens; Benjamin Everton; Sally, Mrs. Charles Richardson.

JEREMIAH RIGGS AND FAMILY.

He came to what is now called Pagetown, in 1800, and married Miss Rachel Keller. They had a large family: William James, Frank, Jeremiah, Jr., George, Elias, Jackson Perry, and three daughters, Rebecca, Nancy and Polly. There is no date of the death of Jeremiah Riggs or his wife. Several of the sons moved to some western states; the daughter, Nancy, never married. Rebecca was married twice, and lived and died in the Hocking Valley. Polly was married to Martin Dye, of Pagetown, for his second wife; left a widow she died at the home of her niece, Mrs. John Crary, in Lebanon township, October 13th, 1895. She was the last one of Jeremiah Riggs family.

JOHN MILES AND FAMILY.

John Miles came from Rutland, Worcester county, Massachusetts, to Cooperstown, N. Y., where he married Chloe Jervis. They came to Belpre, Washington county, Ohio, in 1798, where they remained three years. In 1801 they came to Leading Creek, being the second family in what was afterwards Rutland township. He bought a share in the Ohio Company's Purchase for ninety-six pounds, sterling, and settled on the farm where he died on November 10th, 1847, aged eighty years. Chloe Jarvis Miles died September 21st, 1844. They had seven children. Benjamin Lanson Miles went to Arkansas, had a cotton plantation, some slaves; lived and died there in 1839. He was twice married, but left one son, James B. Miles.

Mary Miles was never married. She died in Rutland, April 9th, 1857, aged sixty-four years.

Barzillai Hosmer Miles was a preacher of the Christian denomination. He married Amy Guthrie, who died leaving two daughters. As a preacher he was successful, traveled some and died of cholera in 1832, while on his way home from Louisiana.

John B. Miles married Mary Johnson and owned a farm in Rutland township, where they lived many years. They had a family of sons and daughters. He died in Racine in 1864, aged sixty-eight years. Mrs. Mary Miles died in Racine, Ohio.

Columbus Miles, son of John and Mary Miles, married Elizabeth Hopkins; was in the marble business at Gallipolis and died there.

Benjamin Harrison Miles, a preacher, and a soldier in the Civil war, but died later. John Wesley Miles, a marble dealer in Gallipolis. Adaline Miles was married to Waid Cross, a merchant in Racine, Ohio. They had a family of sons and daughters. Mrs. Cross died in 1905.

Sally C. Miles was born November 5th, 1803, being the first female born in the township, afterwards Rutland. She was married to Russell Cook, lived on a farm in Rutland. They had a large family of sons and daughters. She died in 1857, aged fifty-four years.

Joseph Jarvis Miles was born October 19th, 1807. He married Sarah Cutler Larkin in 1841. They had children but all died in infancy. He was a tanner by trade, carried on the business in Gallipolis for a number of years, and later in the same business in Pomeroy. He died July 27th, 1855.

Electa Miles, the youngest child of John and Chloe Miles was born August 20th, 1812, and was married to John McQuigg, and lived many years on the "Miles Homestead." They had two children—George McQuigg and Frances. She died January 10th, 1906, aged ninety-four years, loved and esteemed by all.

George McQuigg was born November 25th, 1830. He was married twice, first to Miss Caroline Smith, who was the mother of two children, Lucy M., who died young, and John McQuigg, connected with the Pomeroy National Bank. Miss Kate Edwards was the second wife of Mr. McQuigg. They had three children—Charles, in the salt business as a successor to his father; Anna, married to Mr. Follett, of Kansas, and Emma McQuigg. George McQuigg was a man of affairs, a fine business man, clean in his political actions, genial, affable, always winning the favor of the best citizens. He was general agent of the Ohio Salt Company from 1868 to the time of his death, October 29th, 1892; aged sixty-one years, ten months and twenty-eight days.

Captain James Merrill was a sea-faring man and commanded vessels in the East India trade for Mr. Dexter, a wealthy shipowner and merchant prince. After years of service in Mr. Dexter's employ he quitted the sea and came to Ohio in 1801, settling on a farm in Salem township given to him by Mr. Dexter, but removed to a farm in Rutland township in later years. Capt. Merrill built the first frame house in what is now Meigs county. The weather-boards were of wild cherry, sawed with a whipsaw. He had conducted to the ocean one of the first ships built at Marietta. He was a religious man, highly respected. He died in Rutland, October 29th, 1826.

WILLIAM PARKER, Sr., AND FAMILY.

William Parker, Sr., was born at Malden, Massachusetts, June 5th, 1745, and was married to Mary Warner, January 28th, 1772. She was the daughter of Philemon Warner, of Gloucester, Massachusetts, and was born in 1753. He was a cabinet maker and exported furniture to the West Indies. He bought a share of land in the Ohio Company's Purchase, and left the East in 1789, traveling as far as the forks of the Youghiogheny, where he remained until about 1800; he removed his family to his farm in Salem township, where they lived and reared a large family. Their children were:

Elizabeth Warner, born September 21st, 1773, and died January 19th, 1850, aged seventy-seven years. She was never married and died in Salem.

William, Jr., was born July 4th, 1775, and married Betsy Wyatt, May 13th, 1802. She was a daughter of Deacon Joshua Wyatt.

Sally, born June 6th, 1777, and was married to Judge Ephriam Cutler, April 13th, 1808. She died June 30th, 1846.

John, born June 20th, 1779, and married Lucy Cotton. He was a Halcyon preacher and died in 1849.

Daniel was born August 7th, 1781, and married Priscilla Melloy Ring, October 24th, 1816. He was a preacher of Universal Restoration. He died March 22d, 1861. His wife died September 4th, 1874.

Polly, born May 27th, 1783, and was married to Judge Cushing Shaw. They both lived and died in Salem, leaving a numerous and worthy family of children.

Nancy, born March 13th, 1785, was married to Stephen Strong, Esq. Mr. Strong was an early advocate of temperance. He was elected to the legislature for one term, was a surveyor and held many county offices. They had no children; lived and died in Salem.

Susanna, born March 10th, 1787, was married to Dr. Sylvanus Evarts, and died July 5th, 1815, aged twenty-eight years.

Fanny, born March 26th, 1789, and was married to John Fordyce and had several children. They were farmers and lived and died in Salem.

Ebenezer was born December 22d, 1792, and married Mary Swett, daughter of Benjamin Swett, of Newburyport, Mass.

Ebenezer Parker lived in the old homestead for many years, but sold out and finally removed to Cincinnati to live with his sons, where he died.

Clarissa, born May, 1795, and was married to Peter Shaw. She died May 24th, 1817, aged twenty-two years.

Mr. William Parker, Sr., died November 26th, 1825, and his wife, Mrs. Parker, died February 25th, 1811. They were both members of the Presbyterian Church, lived useful and honorable lives, leaving an exemplary record to their descendants.

The Aleshire brothers, Conrad, Michael and Peter, came as emigrants from the Shenandoah Valley, Virginia, to Ohio, in 1802, and settled first near the mouth of Kiger creek, until 1805, when Michael came to Leading creek and bought a farm, but afterwards moved to Salem, where he died in 1845. Conrad Aleshire came to Leading creek, settled on a farm; had a son, Abram, who came with him from Virginia, who was born in 1784, and who had two children, Anna and Preston Aleshire. Conrad Aleshire died in 1842, aged eighty-nine years. Abram Aleshire died in 1865. Peter Aleshire was a regular Baptist preacher and lived in Salem township.

Thomas Shepherd moved to Leading creek in 1802 and settled on Fraction No. 19, or the Denny lot. He was from Maryland, but married Polly McFarland in Kentucky. She was the daughter of Mr. McFarland, and who was in the Block House in Marietta at the time of the massacre by the Indians of the settlement twelve miles up the Muskingum. In the alarm occasioned by that event the defense of the Block House was left very weak, and Polly McFarland, a girl of sixteen, was given a gun and stationed at a porthole. Mr. McFarland moved to Kentucky, where Polly was married to Thomas Shepherd. Interesting stories are related of her courage in meeting emergencies. One night when Mr. Shepherd had gone to Gallipolis for ammunition, a large bear entered a calf pen not far from the house, and in trying to carry it off the calf bawled, which wakened Mrs. Shepherd, who went out, drove the bear off and up a tree, under which she built a fire and kept it there until morning. It is said of her that another time she was going after the cows in the woods when the dogs treed a raccoon. She sent a boy after an ax, cut down the tree, caught the raccoon, tanned the hide and made herself a pair of shoes.

They had three sons and several daughters. The sons were Charles, Daniel and Thomas. The daughters were, Polly, married to Andrew Long; Nancy, married to Lucius Higley (see Higley family); Sally, married to Mr. Shaw; Jane, Mrs. John Savage; Betsy, Mrs. James Caldwell; Annie; Peggie, Clarissa, Mrs. Backus; Almira, Mrs. Aaron Smith.

Mr. Shepherd's name appears as a voter for the first election for Governor of Ohio; also on the supervisors tax list for 1806, and he was one of the first trustees of Rutland township in 1812. He was born in 1772 and died in 1842.

Caleb Gardner came from the State of New York and settled in Rutland in 1803. He was a man of good business abilities, and served the township in various official capacities with credit to himself and satisfaction to the public. He died November 23d, 1823, aged fifty-nine years.

Joshua Gardner was a son of Caleb Gardner, and was born January 5th, 1793, in Connecticut, and came to Ohio with his father. He also served as constable and other civil offices. He was one of a company who went overland to California in 1849. Returning to Rutland after two years he closed his life in March, 1862, aged seventy-six years and two months.

James E. Phelps came from Connecticut in 1803, and settled in the lower part of Rutland township. He married Phylenda Rice, a sister of Mrs. Daniel Rathburn. Mr. Phelps was an enterprising farmer, filled several township offices, and went to Columbus as a lobby member to get the county of Meigs set off. He was one of the first associate judges of Meigs county. He died in June, 1822. His children: James, who studied medicine, went South and died there; Nancy Phelps was married to William Bing, of Gallia county; Harlow Phelps married Amelia Watkins, and lived in the old homestead; Abel Phelps was a physician, practiced his profession in the lower part of Pomeroy, and died there. He was married twice. His first wife was Ruth Simpson. After her death he married Amy Smith.

John Orlando Phelps was also a doctor and practiced medicine in Piketon, Ohio; afterwards went South and died there. Amelia Phelps was married to Dr. Eli Sigler, who had a considerable practice. They lived near her old home. Dr. Sigler was one of the associate judges at one time of Meigs county. He died May 1st, 1848, aged fifty-three years, ten months and twenty-seven days. He was married twice; his second wife was Barbara Rothgeb, who died April 2d, 1891, aged eighty-two years, two months and four days.

Amanda Phelps died in early womanhood.

DANIEL RATHBURN.

Daniel Rathburn was born in 1767 in Granby, Connecticut, and married Desire Rice, born in 1764, in Connecticut. They came with their family to Leading creek in 1803, and established their home, where itinerant Methodist preachers had regular appointments. The names of Jacob Young, David Young, William Young, James Quinn, James Gilruth, and John P. Kent, and others who found a cordial welcome. Mr. and Mrs. Rathburn were leading and influential citizens in those early times. They had a family of sons—no daughters. Mr. Daniel Rathburn, Sr., died in 1852, aged eighty-five years, six months. Mrs. Rathburn died in 1868, aged ninety-eight years, ten months, three days.

The children were Daniel C. Rathburn, who married Laura Higley, had a farm in Rutland, was justice of the peace, and taught school. They had a numerous family of sons and daughters. He died September 25th, 1855, aged fifty-nine years.

Elisha Rathburn was married to Polly Giles, September 23d, 1819. He came with his father to Ohio and settled on a farm near the village of Rutland. He was highly respected by the community and favorably known as a preacher in the Baptist or Christian denomination. His gifts and graces, zeal and charity were shown in a remarkable degree through a long and useful life.

Elisha Rathburn was born June 30th, 1789, and died August 8th, 1869. Mrs. Rathburn was born April 13th, 1799, and died February 7th, 1896, aged ninety-one years. They had a family of one son, Joseph Newton, and five daughters, Clarissa, Elizabeth, and Roana (Mrs. Seth Paine), and two daughters who died in early womanhood.

Two sons of J. Newton Rathburn, Milton Rathburn and Charles, are successful merchants, and prominent citizens of Meigs county, Milton Rathburn being elected Senator from this district, for state legislature, 1906. They were born and brought up in Rutland township.

Timothy Rathburn, a son of Daniel Rathburn and his wife, Desire Rathburn, married a Miss Daniel, of Gallia county, and

M. E. RATHBURN

EDGAR ERVIN,
Fourth Generation from Daniel Sayre.

lived on a part of the old homestead. They had several children.

Alvin Rathburn was a physician and practiced medicine in Rutland. He was married and had three sons. William P. Rathburn, a banker, removed to Chattanooga, Tennessee, where he was successful in accumulating a large property by investments in iron and coal. He died in Chattanooga.

Joseph Rathburn, son of Alvin, was a physician, as was his brother, James Rathburn, who removed to Gallia county, where he died.

John Rathburn, a son of Daniel Rathburn, Sr., was a doctor, but died young.

Francis Asbury Rathburn was the sixth son of Daniel Rathburn, Sr., and his wife. He was born March 9th, 1800. He was never married but lived with his parents, caring for them with filial devotion in their old age. After the death of his father in 1852 he moved into the village with his mother, where she died in 1863. He continued to live in Rutland until his death, an exemplary man, respected by all who knew him.

Samuel Rathburn was the youngest son of Daniel Rathburn, Sr., and his wife, Desire Rathburn, and was born in 1802. He married a Miss Vanden, of Gallipolis, engaging in the mercantile business in that city. He held several offices of public trust, was probate judge of Gallia county, and maintained an honorable character, a highly respected citizen, until his death.

THE HUNTERS.

An account of hunting adventures, as described by Mr. John Warth and reported by Mr. Silas Jones, who was a member of Mr. Warth's family in 1832. He says that Mr. Warth never tired of entertaining his guests with narratives of perils and adventures in his early life, and Mr. Jones reports, as near as possible, in the actor's own words.

"In the time of great peril, when it was not safe to look out of the fort, and our brother Robert had been shot while chopping a log near the fort, it became necessary to procure some meat for the families in the fort. Thinking the Ohio bottoms less liable to be infested with Indians, George and I stole out of the fort at night, and paddled noiselessly down the river to a point opposite Blannerhasset island, where we hid our canoe in the willows. As soon as it was light we started in different directions to hunt for deer. I had not gone half a mile when I saw two tall savages coming in the direction I was going. I squatted in the high pea vines and thick undergrowth that covered the ground while they passed by near me but did not see me. However, they soon discovered my trail, which they followed back to the canoe, which I supposed they would watch until the owner would come. My great concern now was the safety of my brother George, as he not being aware of the presence of the Indians would return to the canoe and fall a prey to them. Then I decided on a plan to save George, which was to proceed to a point out of sight of the Indians, hide my gun, swim across the river, then swim to the island and watch for George's return. This plan I fully carried out. Along in the afternoon I heard the report of my brother's gun after which my anxiety amounted to agony—minutes seemed hours. At length I saw George coming out of the woods with the carcass of a deer on his back. He looked up and down the shore, when I got his attention and by signs and gestures got him to take in the situation. We both regained the fort without further trouble. When the danger was over I went with a party and recovered my gun and the canoe.

"Another time George and I went out in search of game, and were separated some distance, when I heard the report of his gun, after which I heard cries of distress coming from George. I ran to him with all the possible speed of my limbs, and found him pinned to the earth by a large elk. I was so exhausted that I could not draw the bead, so I ran up and thrust the muzzle of my rifle against the animal's ribs and fired, when he fell dead at my feet. My brother was not much hurt, the horns of the elk had not penetrated through the ample folds of his hunting shirt, which held him to the ground. (The hunter's shirt was made sufficiently large so that he could stow a week's provisions above the belt.) George had fired on the elk, only wounding him, and so enraging the beast that he turned on the hunter and compelled George to take refuge in a high upturned root where he fought with his clubbed rifle till he had nothing left but the bent barrel, when the maddened elk finally dislodged him, with the above result. Our capture was a valuable one, but did not compensate for George's gun."

An Encounter With Wolves at Shade River.

George Warth and Peter Niswonger took their rifles and went out for a hunt. After traveling some time they came to a ridge that ran to near the mouth of Shade river, when Warth said to Niswonger, "You go on the bottom on one side of the ridge and I will take the other side and will come together at the end of the ridge on the bank of Shade river." They started thus, but Niswonger got out of the way, and came out above the second ridge. Warth went directly to the river end of the ridge—there sat seven to ten wolves. They showed no alarm at his approach, the largest walked toward him, the others following. He shot the foremost one, and it fell dead. He reloaded his rifle as soon as he could, for the wolves indicated fight. Then he went into the river until the water was up to his hips, and the wolves went in after him. He shot the foremost one through the shoulder and he went back to the water's edge and sat down and looked at him. He defended himself with his empty rifle, broke the stock in many pieces, and then fought them with the empty barrel. He had the advantage of being in the water deep enough to swim the wolves, and he pounded them until they retreated to the edge of the water and sat down on their haunches and looked at him. He dared not go out of the water as he might not be able to fight if they followed him. Soon Niswonger came on the shore opposite the wolves and Warth crossed over to him and told him "not to shoot—we will call it a draw game, neither party whipped." He would not let Niswonger shoot lest they might be attacked. The hunters returned to their homes on Oldtown creek, and next day increased their force and went back to the place of the battle and found two dead wolves but no live ones. (Sketch by Mr. Silas Jones.)

Black bears were numerous in these parts of southern Ohio in the first years of the nineteenth century. Henry Roush, of Letart township, related an incident of his encounter with bears. He said: "I was going out to bring in the cows, and contrary to my usual custom did not take my rifle with me, and while passing along the rear of my neighbor's field of corn I saw two young bears helping themselves to roasting ears. I succeeded in capturing one of them, which began to squall at a furious rate, which brought the mother bear rushing upon me with great fury. I had to drop my prize and run for a high fence which was near, with the angry bear at my heels. After gaining the top of the fence, I seized a stake and beat off my assailants."

Elk were seen, but not in great numbers. Wolves were numerous and very troublesome. It was as common to hear the howl of a wolf in the twilight of an evening as it was to hear the crowing of a cock in the morning. They would answer each other from hill to hill when gathering their pack for the depredations upon the settler's sheep or young cattle. In 1827 a party of road viewers were cutting out a road from Chester, the county seat of Meigs county, to Sterling Bottom, on the Ohio river, and at a certain point lay out a road from this to Oldtown. The viewers were Nehemiah Bicknell, Samuel Bowman and one or two other men. They had progressed only half way from Chester when night came on and they had to spend the night in the woods. They built fires for protection from wolves, whose howling they heard apparently in force, at no great distance, at intervals all night. The men kept the fires burning, but slept little.

Wolves continued to commit depredations on the farmers' sheep in Lebanon township, a gang having dens somewhere about the head of Ground Hog creek and Oldtown creek. An expert trapper named Allen came from Washington county in 1840 and successfully exterminated these wolves.

The panther was often met by the hunter, but was easily killed, as the animal was of a bold, defiant nature, he would climb a tree where he was an easy mark for the hunter's rifle.

Deer were found in great numbers and were a great blessing to the pioner families, who depended for meat upon the wild game. Venison was a choice meat, while the deer's hide was tanned and served to make various articles of apparel. The deer has disappeared from this county. Gray foxes were numerous and were great enemies to poultry raising, but the red fox seems to have superseded the gray, and neither are seen in later years. The raccoon was a great pest, destroying large quantities of corn while in a green state on the stalk. Coon hunting with dogs was a common sport for boys until the animal has disappeared. The opossum and red and gray squirrel remain in limited numbers. (Silas Jones.)

ABEL LARKIN.

Abel Larkin, son of Matthias Larkin, was born in Lancaster, Worcestor county, Massachusetts, August 29th, 1764, and married Susannah Bridges in 1794, in Rutland, Vermont. She was born in Lunenburg, Nova Scotia. Her father, Mr. Bridges, was a surveyor, but started to Massachusetts on a vessel to prepare a place for his family, and the vessel never returned, nor was heard from after sailing. Her mother was a Haskell, and went to Massachusetts with her family, where she died.

Abel Larkin had mills on Otter creek, Vermont, which were swept away by floods. He then started with wife and four children to Ohio, coming to Leading creek in 1804, in June. He was able to obtain a house on Judge Higley's farm, where his family remained four years. Mr. Larkin and Judge Higley were acquainted in Vermont. In 1808 Mr. Larkin moved into his own cabin on the farm he had purchased. Mr. Larkin was the first township clerk for Salisbury township, elected July 27th, 1805; was also elected justice of the peace in 1808, again in 1812, and again in 1818. Afterwards he served as associate judge for Meigs county.

Their children were four sons and five daughters.

Susannah, born in Vermont in 1796, and died in Rutland in July, 1805.

Emeline Larkin, born in Vermont 1798, and died in Rutland, Ohio, in May, 1824, aged twenty-six years.

Abel Larkin, Jr., was born April 21st, 1801, married Adeline Hadley in Illinois, near Mt. Sterling, in 1835. He settled on a farm in Brown county, where they reared a numerous family —five sons and four daughters. Three of his sons enlisted in the Civil war, and one came back alive with injuries from which he died. He was John Larkin. The daughters were grown to womanhood, married and moved to different parts of the country. Mrs. Adeline Larkin died in 1881. Mr. Abel Larkin, Jr., died in 1884 in Illinois. He had been a pioneer in Ohio, and going to Illinois in 1829, was a pioneer in that state.

Julia Larkin was born June 29th, 1802, in Rutland, Vermont, and removed with her parents to Leading creek in 1804. She was married to Nehemiah Bicknell March 16th, 1826, and came with him to Lebanon township, to his farm, where she lived until her death, February 25th, 1863. They had six children, one son and five daughters.

Stillman Carter Larkin was born in Rutland, Ohio, March 9th, 1808. He married Mary Hedrick, November 21st, 1837, and lived on the Larkin homestead until death. Stillman C.

The Larkin Homestead—One Hundred Years in the Family.

Larkin died in January, 1898, aged ninety years, ten months, twenty-three days. Mary Larkin died May 30th, 1904, aged ninety-two years, five months, fifteen days. They had no children.

Sarah Cutler Larkin was born September 6th, 1811, in Rutland, Ohio, and was married to Joseph Jervis Miles, April 12th, 1841. They lived in Gallipolis a few years, then came to Pomeroy, where Mr. Miles died in July, 1855. Mrs. Miles returned to the old Larkin homestead. She had no children that lived. Her death occurred January 17th, 1895, at the age of eighty-three years, four months, eleven days.

Curtis Larkin was born May 27th, 1813, in Rutland, Ohio. He was in California a few years, but returned to Rutland, Ohio, where he married Lura Hubbell, who died in 1846. He married again—Sarah Church. They had one son, George B. Larkin. Their home was always in Rutland, Ohio. Mr. Larkin held some local and township offices, was a trustee of Rutland township several years. He was a member of the First Christian church and served as an active local elder for more than thirty years.

Edwin Larkin was born September 25th, 1815, in Rutland, Ohio. He went to the South in 1839 and never returned.

Betsy Larkin was born August 8th, 1806, in Salisbury township, Gallia county. She was married to Daniel Cutler, November 5th, 1834. They lived in Warren township, Washington county, Ohio, for twenty-one years, and had two children, Charles Curtis and Mary, who died when sixteen years of age. Mr. and Mrs. Cutler moved to the West in 1856, and settled finally in Franklin county, Kansas. Mrs. Cutler died June 19th, 1883, aged nearly seventy-seven years.

Daniel Cutler was born February 19th, 1799, in Waterford, Washington county, Ohio. He was the son of Judge Ephram Cutler and his first wife, who died early, leaving four children, Charles, Nancy, Mary, and Daniel, who was taken to the home of Rev. Manasseh Cutler, where he spent his childhood.

His father, Ephram Cutler, married Sarah Parker, and she was the mother of Hon. William P. Cutler. Mr. Daniel Cutler was an anti-slavery man, and lived in Kansas in those exciting times of border warfare. He was also a temperance man, and a member of the Congregational church. He was the first postmaster of Rantoul, Franklin county, was a farmer, owned a thousand acres of land in one body. He lived and died an honorable, Christian gentleman, on January 10th, 1887. Charles C. Cutler, an only child, survives him and occupies the homestead.

Mr. Daniel Cutler commenced life in the Northwestern Territory, and followed up along the border of civilization during a most eventful period of time, for the whole of his eighty-eight years of life.

Abel Larkin, whose family has been noted, died February 17th, 1830, in Rutland, Ohio, aged sixty-five years, five months, nineteen days.

Susannah Larkin (Bridges) died August 14th, 1860, aged eighty-nine years, four months, twenty-six days. She passed away from her own homestead in Rutland, a woman honored.

Nehemiah Bicknell was the son of Japhet Bicknell and wife, Amy Bicknell (nee Burlingame), was born June 26th, 1796, at East Greenwich, Rhode Island. His parents moved to New York state in 1798, where he lived until nineteen years of age, and his father and brother having died, Nehemiah, with his widowed mother, came with a company under the leadership of Rev. Samuel Porter, to Athens, Ohio, in October, 1815. They traveled with teams and covered wagons, and were forty days on the way, always stopping over Sunday. His mother died in February, 1816, and lies buried in the old cemetery at Athens, leaving him and his younger sister, Zimrode, alone among strangers in a new country. God took care of them and they soon found good friends.

March 16th, 1826, Nehemiah Bicknell married Julia Larkin, in Rutland, Ohio, and they moved immediately to make their home on his farm in Lebanon township on the banks of the Ohio river. They endured many hardships incident to pioneer life, none of which they deprecated more than the ignorance and low state of morals in the neighborhood. Mr. Bicknell opened his own house for preaching in about 1828 or 1829, to the Methodist itinerant. Later he secured the building of a school house on his land adjoining the Pioneer burying ground, where the preaching appointment was removed, and continued for many years. Afterward he gave a lot for a site for a church, deeded to trustees of the Methodist Episcopal church, and a public graveyard. Mr. Bicknell was a public spirited man, who felt the lack of early education a constant impediment to progress. He was elected magistrate three terms, township trustee, postmaster eleven years, Sunday-school superintendent for many years, class leader when the appointment was known as the Oldtown class. He was an uncompromising temperance man all of his long life, and erected a large barn, the second building in Meigs county raised without the compliment of whisky. He was a road viewer and helped in laying out roads in nearly every part of the county, and dissented from the policy of narrow minded men who would lay out a public road on inaccessable hillsides, or around the corner of a selfish man's farm. He claimed for the traveling public suitable ground, and making good roads everywhere. At eighty-three years of age his step was firm, his eyes bright, and cheeks rosy. His birthday, celebrated in June, 1879, he, with his eldest daughter, left home August 1st to revisit his boyhood home in Chenango county, New York, and attend to the placing of gravestones anew at his father's grave. In some strange manner he seemed to have gone out of the car to the platform, when he fell off and was killed. This was on the Erie railroad, near Beaver Flats, and the fatality occurred about 3 a. m., August 6th, 1879. His stricken daughter brought his body back and he was laid by the side of his wife in the graveyard by the little church called "Bicknell's Chapel." (E. L. B.)

The children of Nehemiah Bicknell and his wife, Julia Bicknell (nee Larkin), were Emeline Larkin, born February 19th, 1827, and was married to Isaac A. Cowdery in July, 1846. It proved a most unfortunate marriage, and she obtained a divorce in June, 1853, in the Common Pleas court of Meigs county, and her name restored to that of Bicknell. She had borne two children, a son, dying at three months, and a daughter, Ella Frances, who died October 10th, 1860, in her ninth year.

Julia Amy was born December 28th, 1828, and died of fever, September, 1846.

An infant son of Nehemiah Bicknell and his wife, March 10th, 1833.

Zimrode Adaline was married to John Roberts in May, 1855. She died December 10th, 1870, leaving three children, Arthur B., Zimrode Ella, and Albert John Roberts.

Sarah Elizabeth, born September 24th, 1839, and died October 3d, 1860.

Mary Susannah, born March 7th, 1842, was married to Rev. George J. Conner in October, 1869. They had one son, Charlie Cookman, but father and son both died—the first 1873, the latter 1876. She was again married to David B. Cross in January, 1879, and died March 7th, 1882, forty years of age. She left one son, Willie Bicknell Cross.

Allen Ogden was born in Maryland, April 13th, 1775. He was in Marietta in 1788. In June, 1795, he married Miss Hannah Keller, with whom, in April, 1804, they moved to what is now known as Columbia township, Meigs county. He purchased land, cleared up a farm, where he made his home and reared a family of ten children. He served many years as a justice of the peace, and filled other responsible township offices.

Mary Ogden was married to Joshua Wood, the first couple married in Columbia township. They had nine children. Mr. Wood was a justice of the peace and Whig politician.

Margaret Wood married Elias P. Davis. She died, leaving two children. Nancy Wood was married to Nehemiah Bobo. They had eleven children, twenty-nine grand children and five great-grandchildren.

William Wood married Sarah Rutherford and reared four children, with a number of descendants.

Elizabeth Wood was married to Eli Vale, and they had a large family of children and grandchildren.

Joshua Wood married Elizabeth Forrest, and they had one child.

Rachel Wood was married to J. Q. A. Vale, a physician. Their home was in Minnesota. Dr. Vale has been a member of the legislature of that state. They had six children.

Mary Wood married Levi Whitlock, and they went to Minnesota and had a large family of children.

Adah Ogden, daughter of Alvin Ogden and wife, was born March 7th, 1799, and was married to John Conner. They moved to Indiana. To them were born six children.

Sabert Ogden was born October 3d, 1801, married Eliza Forrest, and settled in Salem. They had seyen children. Sabert Ogden died February 10th, 1874. Mrs. Ogden died December 24th, 1896, aged eighty-five years, six months, eighteen days.

Alvin Ogden, Jr., married Nancy Jordan, and resided in Salem. They had two children, and several grandchildren.

Herbert Ogden had three sons in the Civil war, Alvin, John, and Hugh. John was in Company I, Fifty-third Ohio Volunteer Infantry, and died in the service at Camp Denison, Ohio.

Hugh Ogden, the second son of Alvin Ogden, Sr., was born March 11th, 1804. He never married. He died in 1872 in Salem township.

Nancy Ogden, daughter of Alvin Ogden, Sr., and his wife, was born May 18th, 1806. She was married to William Green, and they both lived and died in Columbia township. They had five children. Albert Green was a soldier in the Eighteenth Ohio Volunteer Infantry, and died in the service.

Lovina Ogden Green married Lewis Castor, of Columbia. Hannah Green married Miles Graham, a member of the Eighteenth Ohio Volunteer Infantry, who died shortly after the close of the war.

Cynthia Green married William Graham, who was a soldier and died in the service the first year of the Civil war.

Elizabeth Ogden, daughter of Alvin Ogden, Sr., was born July 25th, 1808, and was married to Daniel Caleb, and moved to Hardin county, Ohio, where they died. They had four children and numerous descendants.

Noah Ogden, a son of Alvin Ogden, Sr., was born March 16th, 1811. He married Dorcas Graham and settled in Salem township and had four children, and numerous descendants. He died in 1890.

Alvin Ogden, Sr., died January 4th, 1867, aged nearly ninety-two years. He was a son of a Revolutionary soldier, himself a pioneer of Meigs county. When he died he left ten children, 129 grandchildren, and seven great-grandchildren. No race suicide in his posterity.

The foregoing sketch is copied from a history of the Ogden family, as a part of that interesting narrative published in the "Telegraph," January 28th, 1898. S. C. Larkin.

Shubael Nobles and family came from Tremont township, Rutland county, Vermont, to Marietta in 1801. Then to the Joel Higley farm in 1804, and finally to his own farm in the northwest corner of Section No. 15, in Rutland, in 1805.

Mrs. Nobles before marriage was Elizabeth Post. They had three sons and six daughters. Mr. Nobles was a tanner by trade, also a shoemaker. Charles F. Nobles, a son, was a blacksmith. He married Sarah Fanny Winn in October, 1818. She was a daughter of Abraham Winn, and was born July 24th, 1795, in Ontario county, New York. She was a noble woman, with great energy. They reared a large family of sons and daughters. Mr. Charles F. Nobles died in 1870. Mrs. Nobles died November 24th, 1890, aged ninety-five years, four months.

Lewis Nobles, son of Shubael Nobles, married Betsy Strausburg. He was noted as an ingenious mechanic. He died May 26th, 1887, aged sixty-seven years, eleven months, seven days. His wife died March 1st, 1897, in her seventy-sixth year of age.

Osmar Nobles was never married, but lived on the old farm

Silas Nobles went to Indiana, married and died there.

Abigail Nobles, daughter of Shubael Nobles, was married to Phineas Matthews, of Gallia county. Julia married Jacob A. Winn, lived in Rutland, and died in 1882, at the age of eighty-five years. Eliza was married to Jacob Swisher and lived in Gallia county.

Esther Nobles was married to Abel Chase, of Rutland, Ohio. She was born March 26th, 1808. Eunice Nobles died March 17th, 1878, aged seventy-eight years. Mary Nobles died in Rutland, aged sixty-one years. Shubael Nobles, Sr., died in 1854, aged ninety-one years. His wife died in 1855, aged eighty-eight years.

William Parker, second, was born in Newburyport, Massachusetts, July 4th, 1775, and came to Marietta with his father, William Parker, first, in 1798. He married Betsy Wyatt, daughter of Deacon Joshua Wyatt, of Athens county, May 13th, 1802, and they came to Rutland, Ohio, in 1804, and settled on a farm, which has been owned and occupied by a Parker for more than one hundred years.

The children of William Parker, second, and his wife were: Eliza, who was married to Samuel Halliday, and lived in Meigs county. They had a family of sons and daughters; Alexander died when a child; William Halliday; Jane was Mrs. Robbins; Samuel Halliday married Elizabeth Remington, of Pomeroy; Eliza, Henry, Thomas, Edwin, and Mary left Meigs county with their parents in 1850.

William Parker, third, married Lovina Stout. Their children were: William Parker, fourth, Mary, Ida, Sophronia, Edwin Parker, Barton, and Sarah—Mrs. Green, who died early, leaving one daughter. Edwin married and lives in Cincinnati. Ida Parker was a successful teacher in the public schools in Middleport, Ohio. Two brothers and two unmarried sisters live together in the homestead.

Silas Parker, son of William Parker, second, studied medicine and went to the West when quite a young man.

Mary Parker was married to Buckingham Cooley, who died early, leaving a widow and one daughter. Mrs. Cooley was married afterwards to William Bartlett, of Athens, Ohio.

Sarah E. Parker became the wife of Tobias A. Plantz, Esq., and lived in Pomeroy. They had two children, Mary E. Plants who died young, and George Wyatt Plantz, banker and prominent citizen of Pomeroy for many years, identified with all good enterprises for the prosperity of the town. He married Mary G. Daniel, daughter of H. G. Daniel, banker and an esteemed business man of Pomeroy. They have one son, who bears the family name, Wyatt Garfield Plantz, and is one of the bankers—"First Citizens Bank," of Pomeroy.

John Wyatt Parker, son of William Parker, second, and his wife, was born in Rutland. He married Eliza McQuigg, and lived in Gallipolis for several years, was auditor of Gallia county, but removed to Dubuque, Iowa.

The Parker Homestead—One Hundred and Five Years in the Family.

Daniel Parker, son of William Parker, second, and his wife, was born October 22d, 1809. He married Catharine E. Gillespie, of Dayton, Ohio, in 1847. They had three sons: George G., Daniel Herbert, and Frank H. Parker, all noted physicians and specialists in surgery. Mr. Daniel Parker owned and occupied the homestead, and died January 19th, 1893, aged eighty-three years, two months, twenty-eight days. Mrs. Parker died in 1908, in her eighty-fourth year, a woman of rare accomplishments, one who never grew old.

This Parker homestead is occupied by Dr. Frank Parker, the only surviving member of his father's family.

A party of Indians came to Rutland sometime in the interval between 1804 and 1808. The date is not as certain as the incident. It was a custom in those days when preaching by a minister was only occasional, to observe the Sabbath by services at the home of some family in the neighborhood. One Sunday when the meeting was in progress, Indians were seen looking through the cracks of the door, and between the logs. Immediately consternation prevailed, the women crying and wringing their hands, while some of the men went to the door, shook hands with them and found them to be friendly. The Indians said they wanted "johnny-cake," which fortunately was at hand, so the request was granted and the Indians departed. Mr. Milo Higley has written a very good song on johnny-cake, and we venture to copy two stanzas relating to the foregoing narrative.

"It was Sunday in that early day,
And all had gone to church
In the house of Mr. Larkin,
God's holy book to search.
Around the fireside they met,
A blessing to partake,
While from the hearth came up the fume
Of steaming johnny-cake.

"While thus in solemn worship there
The women gave a scream,
For through a crack in the cabin wall
A red-skin's eyes were seen.
The stately deacons rose and asked,
'Why this disturbance make?'
In Indian language they replied,
'We want some johnny-cake!'"

This visit was the last one of the Indians in the vicinity of Rutland.

PIONEER SOCIETY.

A meeting preliminary to a call for the organizing of a pioneer society met at the court house in Pomeroy in October, 1876, Mr. H. B. Smith, chairman, Aaron Stivers, secretary. Those present were Stillman C. Larkin, Aaron Torrence, Nehemiah Bicknell, Silas Jones, Mrs. H. B. Smith, Mrs. S. C. Miles, and Mrs. E. L. Bicknell. They met and proceeded to name a committee to announce the time and place for a regular organization of the Meigs County Pioneer Society, and to prepare a constitution, with suitable by-laws, for the future conduct of the society. They reported at the next meeting, which was held in the court house at Pomeroy, November 1st, 1876, pursuant to the call of the last meeting.

President Stillman C. Larkin in the chair, and Aaron Stivers, secretary. The object of the meeting was stated by the president and then the report and constitution was read and adopted.

"In view of the fact that all of the first settlers of Meigs county have passed away, and most of their children are also gone, and that time is effacing the mementos and monuments that have marked the only history of our county, we are admonished that unless immediate steps are taken to preserve the remembrance of those interesting events they will be forgotten and lost. In order therefore to recover and preserve and record the past and current history of our county for the benefit and satisfaction of our present population, as well as those whom it may interest when time shall have removed us who now record these events, this society is formed and for its regulation have adopted the following constitution:

"Article 1. This society shall be known as the Meigs County Pioneer Society.

"Art. 2. The object of this society shall be the promotion of social intercourse, the collection and preservation of the history of the early settlers of Meigs county, and such other matters of interest as may be declared by the society to be worthy of record and preservation.

"Art. 3. Any person who has been twenty years a resident of Meigs county, and is over fifty years of age, or who is the wife of a member, may become a member of this society by signing this constitution, and all male members paying into its treasury five cents, and fifty cents annually during membership. Residents of adjoining counties may become members by a vote of the society.

"Art. 4. The officers of the society shall consist of a president, vice-president, treasurer, corresponding secretary, and recording secretary, and an executive committee of five, who shall hold their respective offices for the term of one year, and until their successors are elected and installed.

"Art. 5. The officers shall be elected annually by ballot on the day of the annual meeting, and a majority of the members present and voting shall be necessary to a choice.

"Art. 6. The annual meeting of this society shall be held on the second Thursday in August of each year. The president or executive committee may call a meeting at discretion.

"Art. 7. All money must be paid to the recording secretary, who shall pay the same to the treasurer, taking his receipt for the same.

"Art. 8. The treasurer shall deposit the funds of the society in some solvent bank in the name of the society, and pay the same out on the order of the recording secretary, as directed by the executive committee, unless otherwise ordered by the society.

"Art. 9. A majority of the members present at an annual meeting shall determine the place of the next annual meeting thereafter to be holden.

"Art. 10. The executive committee with the two secretaries shall give the necessary notice, and make arrangements for the annual meeting of the society.

"Art. 11. The constitution may be altered or amended at any annual meeting by a vote of two-thirds of all the members present."

The Signers of the Constitution.

Horace Holt, Mary Lasher, N. Bicknell, Sarah C. Miles, Benjamin Smith, P. Pennington, Samuel Bradbury, Samuel Halliday, Sarah Murphy, Samuel S. Paine, Mary Simms, Sophrina Stivers, Silas Jones, W. Stivers, John Erwin, Electa McQuigg, Aaron Thompson, Sarah F. Nobles, Aaron Stivers, Persis O. Cooper, T. A. Plants, Stillman C. Larkin, S. Bosworth, W. A. Barringer, John Ruble, L. Smith, Geo. W. Cooper, W. B. Smith, W. B. Pennington, John C. Hysell.

The society then proceeded to choose officers and the following were elected:

Stillman C. Larkin, president; John C. Hysell, vice-president; H. B. Smith, treasurer; Aaron Stivers, recording secretary; Geo. W. Cooper, corresponding secretary; Samuel Bradbury, Silas Jones, Washington Stivers, Aaron Thompson, and John Ervin, executive committee.

It was then determined by a vote of the society to hold the next annual meeting in Middleport.

The meeting then adjourned.

STILLMAN C. LARKIN, President.
AARON STIVERS, Secretary.

Benjamin Smith, who was born in Salisbury township in 1804, gave some items, related interesting incidents of early times, and promised if life and health permitted to prepare a paper for the annual meeting, as his father and grandfather were among the first early settlers in the county.

John C. Hysell gave incidents of early history and consented to write an article from his knowledge of pioneer events.

Samuel Halliday, who came from Scotland in 1819, and was county auditor for twenty-three years, expressed his gratification at this moment, and made some very appropriate remarks in relation to it. He also promised to furnish a paper containing a history of events in the county, and observations on the conduct of county affairs.

T. A. Plantz spoke of a history prepared by a son of Daniel Parker, who lived in Clermont county, that included valuable information of the earliest settlements in Meigs county, and he would secure a copy for this pioneer society.

H. B. Smith offered the following resolution, which was adopted: "Resolved, that each member of this society be requested to furnish in a written form, at the next annual meeting, such information as shall be within the meaning and spirit of the constitution of this society, and that T. A. Plantz be appointed a committee to procure the Parker papers."

A paper was filed containing an account of the settlement of N. Bicknell in 1820, in Lebanon township.

SKETCH OF EARLY HISTORY.

By Luther Hecox.

Thurman Hecox and family moved from the Whetstone, New York, to Newbury in Ohio, between the Big Hocking and Little Hocking rivers in August, 1800, and the same year moved up the Hocking river four miles into Troy township.

The next year, 1801, they planted corn on the George Ackley farm and one day when they were hoeing corn they killed five rattlesnakes, not until Mr. Hecox had been bitten by one. They had to go up the Muskingum river four miles above Marietta to a floating mill in summer; in winter they lived on boiled corn and turnips. Their meat was venison. The nearest neighbor was Mr. Humphrey, who lived on what is known as Waterman's hill. Another neighbor was Mr. Sutton, a trapper. In 1803 they moved to the middle branch of Shade river, to No. 4, in Troy township. They moved with an ox sled and two yoke of oxen, the first team that ever went through Tupper's Plains. David Daily drove the hogs, and as they tired out he had to camp in the woods with them to keep the wolves from killing them. David Daily was a Revolutionary soldier. Nathan Burris was the first family to settle on the middle branch of Shade river, one mile above where Levi Stedman built his first mill. Solomon Burris, an uncle to Nathan Burris, lived there. Mr. Longworth and Mr. Stone settled on Congress land, and Jacob Cowdery settled on the middle branch, at the mouth of the west branch of Shade river, above Stedman's mill. Levi Stedman and Peter Grow lived in Gallia county, half a mile below the line between the two counties. Afterward they got one section annexed to Athens county, which then ran no farther than the Orange township line, with the exception of one section which belonged to Gallia county. This line runs east to the Ohio river, near the mouth of a small stream called Indian run. Samuel Branch came next with his family and located on the east side of the middle branch of Shade river, and Ezra Hoyt came about the same time. Jacob Rice settled on the west side of the west branch in 1806. Mr. Kingsbury took land on the first fork of the west branch of Shade river, which is known as Kingsbury, after the name of the first settler. He was a brother-in-law to Levi Stedman. The first organization of militia was in 1805. Thurman Hecox was elected captain and Joseph Guthrie first lieutenant. He lived in No. 5. Jacob Halsey and a man named Lasley lived on the middle branch of Shade river. They hauled grain to the mouth of Hocking, there loaded in canoes and pushed up to the floating mill on the Muskingum river above Marietta, a trip that took nine days to go and return. There were no stores nearer than Marietta or Gallipolis. Prices were high—sixty-two and one-half cents for prints, the same for brown sheeting, and tea was two dollars a pound. Bears, panthers, wolves and deer were plenty, also small game. Wild turkeys were seen in flocks of hundreds. Mr. Hecox killed a bear that weighed four hundred pounds when dressed. William and Jeptha Hecox were in the woods and treed a half-grown bear. Jeptha ran home to get an ax, or a gun, and left William and the dogs to watch the bear. While he was gone the bear came down the tree, the dogs seized him, and William took a pine knot and struck him in the head and killed him. Levi Stedman had his hog pen near his house and one night he was away and a bear came into the pen to get a hog, but Mrs. Stedman threw a firebrand at him from the window and frightened him away. Cyrus Cowdery killed an elk, the last one seen in these parts. John Sloan was hunting deer one day when his dogs treed a panther. He shot and wounded it, when it came at him; the dogs caught hold, and Sloan declares that he "shot the animal nine times before he killed it." In the year 1804 Mr. Hecox bought a pair of hand-mill stones, on which they ground wheat and corn, and sifted it through a buckskin sieve. Levi Stedman built a log mill on what is now Chester, and put Mr. Hecox's hand-mill stones in his mill until he could get larger ones. These pioneers had to go to the Scioto river to obtain salt, a journey of seventy miles, and paid two dollars a bushel for the salt. There was only a horse-path for travel, and carried by pack horses the salt, the party camping out at night. Later roads were made for the use of carts and oxen. They went to Marietta for all mail matter until 1812. There was a mail route opened from Parkersburg to Point Pleasant running through by Stedman's Mill. Levi Stedman was appointed Postmaster, he was also the first Justice of the Peace, and Thurman Hecox was Constable. These men filled these offices for a number of years, without opposition. Levi Stedman opened a store, carried on farming, ran a saw and grist mill, kept a tavern, and owned a distillery. Wool had to be carded, spun and woven by hand, flax was raised, and manufactured into cloth, for wearing apparel. Some men had suits of dressed deerskin. The first preaching was at Nathan Burris' house, and next by Rev. Eli Stedman at Samuel Branch's. Afterwards they had occasional preaching by different denominations. In 1820, Elisha Rathburn was the preacher, and a goodly number experienced religion and united with the Bible Christian Church. The first schoolhouse was built on Samuel Branch's land, and the first teacher there was a Miss Pratt, who lived on Pratt's fork, a mile up the river. William and Benjamin Bellows were settlers in this neighborhood, until William sold out to Caleb Cartwright, a preacher of the Seventh Day Baptist.

The name of Stedman occurs so frequently that an explanation is in order. From Walker's History of Athens, we take the statement: "Alexander Stedman, a native of Vermont, and by profession an artisan, settled in Rome township in 1804. In 1805, he was appointed a Judge of the Court of Common Pleas, and served in that position several years. One of his sons was Eli Stedman, a minister. Another son was Levi Stedman, a Commissioner of Athens county, and for a short time in Meigs. Bial Stedman married Sally Foster in 1811," and had sons and daughters. Capt. Julius C. Stedman, a son of Bial Stedman, was a soldier in the Mexican War, and a soldier in 116th Ohio V. I. from the first to the close of the Civil War. He always had a home in or near Athens.

EXTRACT FROM J. H. STEWART'S SKETCH OF LONG BOTTOM.

Long Bottom is situated in the eastern part of Meigs county. The first settlers were Thomas Rairdon and the Colmans, probably before 1800, as the date is not positively known. William Buffington bought land in 1808, and several families came about that time, the Whitesides, Collins' and others. Thomas Rairdon built the first grist mill in 1815. The first postoffice was kept on the Warner farm in 1815. Robert Collins, Postmaster. The first Methodist Church was built in 1844. The first Christian Church in 1847, and the first store was kept by John Roberts and William Hicks in 1839, near the mouth of Forked Run. J. H. Stewart came to Long Bottom in 1830. The leading business of the place has been the working up of the splendid forest into staves, and the manufacture of various kinds of casks. In 1819, this locality was an almost unbroken forest."

Lebanon township was formed in 1813, taken out of Letart township, and possesses a greater river boundary than any other township in Meigs county. It was a dense forest at the time of its organization. Trees of great size, and timber of the finest quality, covered the rich bottom lands of the Ohio river and the creeks of Old Town and Groundhog, while the hills bore the best yellow pine and spruce for lumber. The sugar maple, hickory, black oak and white oak, poplar, beech and sycamore excelled in size and quality any forests of Europe. The black walnut, white walnut and wild cherry were favorite woods for the manufacture of furniture, and for inside work of the best houses. Black walnut and cherry were used particularly for the making of coffins in those early days. So these trees of Lebanon had special attractions to the commercial eyes of later emigrants. More than one farm was paid for by the cordwood cut and sold to steamboats for fuel, when steamboats first ran on the Ohio river. Besides the trees, were growths of wild fruits, crab apples, red and black hawes, raspberries and blackberries, and two or three varieties of grapes, and not least in profusion, beauty or lusciousness, was the papaw. There were herbs and roots used for medicinal purposes, and collected to sell for money. Ginseng, snakeroot and nervine, or ladies' slipper, grew in abundance in the shade of the great trees. Two remarkable trees are worthy of notice. One, a monster sycamore on Old Town creek not far from the mouth of the stream. It was hollow, and made a home for a family once, afterwards served as a stable for horses. The other tree was a sycamore, and hollow, and stood on the bottom land of N. Bicknell's farm in Great Bend.

Dr. Philip Lauck and Rev. Ezra Grover came from Eastern Virginia with their families in 1813 and bought a fine tract of land in Lebanon township, on the Ohio river bottom. Rev. Grover was a Methodist preacher, but was superannuated from the Baltimore Conference. Dr. Lauck was his son-in-law by marriage and had an extensive and successful practice, which took him away from home much of the time, so that the care of his growing family, and of the making of a farm out of the wilderness developed upon Father Grover and Mrs. Lauck. Rev. Grover was a good preacher, a zealous Christian and an able defender of the faith, as held by Methodism. They opened their door for public preaching, and many a weary itinerant was cheered by their hospitality. Dr. Lauck died comparatively young, leaving a widow and six children. The sons, Isaac, Ezra, and Simon; the daughters, Mary Ann, Hannah and Elizabeth. Isaac Lauck married Nancy Hall, and Ezra Lauck married her sister, Rachel Hall, of Old Town. They moved to Missouri many years ago. Mary Ann Lauck died of consumption in early womanhood, Hannah Lauck married Nicholas Richardson, son of a Scotch family who came to Sterling Bottom. Elizabeth Lauck was married to James

Amsden, a highly respected man, who took charge of the farm, and the family after the death of Father Grover in 1835.

In 1811, a company of Scotch from Glasgow, Scotland, through the influence of Nahum Ward of the Ohio Company's Land Purchase, emigrated to Ohio, and settling on Sterling Bottom, named for the "land of the heather." George Richardson, the Pattersons, McCoys and others. Dissatisfaction, discontent, homesickness and death served to break up and scatter the company. Only Mr. George Richardson remained, and he was a merchant and capable of adapting himself to the primitive conditions of the country. Mrs. Richardson was a native of Antigua, one of the British West Indies, and had inherited slaves and plantation interests, but England freed the slaves, and much of the riches vanished. They had a family, one daughter, Eliza Richardson. Nicholas Richardson, the eldest son, married Hannah Lauck. George, Jr., and other children names unknown. The Richardsons left Sterling Bottom some time in the 30's.

Philip Buffington purchased the Island of Duvol in 1796, ever since known as Buffington's Island. Joseph Buffington came from Hampshire county, Virginia, in 1814, bought a farm, Jacob Buffington also, located on the Ohio bottoms, opposite and below the island. They both had large families of sons and daughters. They were a well-to-do, industrious, hospitable people—good neighbors.

THE PICTURED ROCKS OF ANTIQUITY.

The rock of Antiquity is so called from the fact that the earliest settlers found engraven on its face inscriptions and figures of ancient date. These consisted of names of persons not English; also the figure of an Indian cut in the face of the rock. He was represented as in a squatting position, his right elbow on his knee, with a tomahawk pipe in his mouth. Dr. Fuller Elliot, a man of much learning, thought that these inscriptions were made by a party of Frenchmen who descended the river after the evacuation of Fort Duquesne—now Pittsburg, as the date on the rock seemed to correspond with that event. The inscriptions are now obliterated.

The rock in question is situated about four miles below Letart Falls, and is detached from a confused mass of rocks that have fallen from the cliff above. The village of Antiquity takes its name from this rock.—Silas Jones.

Comments on the Foregoing by Stillman C. Larkin.

The opinion of Judge Elliot (who at an early period lived near the noted rock, and saw the inscriptions), that they were made by a party of Frenchmen, is doubtless correct. But what particular party did the work is not so clear. The English and French nations were contending for many years by diplomacy, and by wars, to secure the title and possession of the Ohio Valley, and were not slack in employing every available means to strengthen their claims. In a history of the Kanawha Valley by Professor V. A. Wilson, is the following:

"In 1748, the British Parliament passed laws authorizing the formation of many new settlements and issuing land grants for the settlement of the upper Ohio. In view of such aggression the Governor General of Canada, by order of his home government, determined to place along the 'Oyo,' or La Belle Riviere, a number of leaden plates suitably inscribed, asserting the claims of France to lands on both sides of the river, even to the source of the tributaries. The command consisted of eight subaltern officers, six cadets, 180 Canadians and 55 Indians, an armorer, 20 soldiers, 270 men in all.

The expedition left Montreal on the 15th of June, 1749, and on the 29th reached the junction of the Monongahela and the Allegheny rivers, where the first plate was buried. The expedition then descended the river depositing plates at the mouths of the principal tributaries, and on the 18th of August they reached the mouth of the Great Kanawha and on the point between the rivers the fifth plate was buried. It was found in 1846 by a son of John Beale of Mason county, West Virginia, and was removed from the spot where it had lain for ninety-seven years.

From the mouth of the Great Kanawha the voyage was continued down the river depositing plates until they reached the mouth of the Great Miami, where they buried the sixth and last plate, August 30th, 1749, and returned to Montreal by way of Maumee." It being the business of this company to establish monuments of ownership, it seems reasonable to suppose that they might have made the inscriptions on the rock at Antiquity, a historic monument worthy of giving name to that enterprising village of Antiquity. S. C. L.

Dr. Fuller Elliot was the son of Aaron Elliot and wife Lydia, and was born in Sutton, Massachusetts. He was a university graduate, and chose the profession of medicine. Fuller Elliot was an agent, and possibly a stockholder in the Ohio Company's Purchase, as the county records show his name in the making of deeds of lands in 1792 to purchasers of lands situated in Washington and Gallia counties. He entered land for himself in 1805, 277 acres, and again in 1817, 648 acres in Letart township.

Fuller Elliot was a man of high character and rare attainment, and locating in Letart at that early date; was prominent in helping to organize townships, and in all matters pertaining to public interest and benefit. He was appointed Associate Judge of Gallia, and afterwards of Meigs county. He was elected to the Legislature of Ohio, in all offices serving with fidelity to the people, and honor to himself. He married a daughter of Seth Jones who lived near, and came to Letart about the same time. Judge Elliot and wife had a large family. Mary Elliot, the eldest daughter, was born June 7, 1803, and was married to John Weldon. Mrs. Weldon spent most of her married life not far from her father's home, and reared a numerous family. Serena Elliot, another daughter, married —— Swearingen and moved to West Virginia.

Decatur S. Elliot married Parma Sherwood, and resided in West Virginia, Graham Station. They had a number of children. Decatur Elliot and two or three of his sons were soldiers in the Civil War to preserve the Union.

Philip Elliot, a son of Fuller Elliot, married Serena Myers, and had four children—Martha, Eliza, Thornton J. and Benjamin. He had served as lieutenant in the militia, but died young.

Thornton J. Elliot, a son of Philip Elliot, served in the Civil War, and won honorable distinction and promotions for bravery and irreproachable conduct during the War for the Union.

In his later life Judge Elliot resumed the practice of medicine until his death which occurred in 1832, at the age of 60 years.

James Smith, Sr., removed from Marietta, and located above the mouth of Leading Creek in the spring of 1797. He died May 8th, 1817. His wife was Elizabeth Mack, who died August 9th, 1821, aged 77 years. He was 73 years of age.

Their children were: Benjamin Smith, Esq., born October 1st, 1770, and married Alma Barker, a daughter of Judge Isaac Barker, of Athens, O.

Their children were five sons and four daughters.

Benjamin Smith, Sr., died August 7th, 1836, aged 66 years.

Mrs. Smith died August 29th, 1831, aged 54 years 8 months 11 days.

John, James, Benjamin, Barker and Sardine (the sons, and Polly, Elizabeth, Catharine and Rhoda and Amy, daughters), of Benjamin Smith, Sr.

John N. Smith lived and died in Middleport, Meigs county.

James Smith married Eliza Murray, of Rutland, and emigrated to Arkansas where they both died.

Benjamin Smith, second, a native of Salisbury, born in 1814, and died on May 12th, 1887, aged 83 years.

Barker Smith settled on the West Branch of Thomas Fork creek.

Sardine Smith lived on Hysell run.

Polly Smith was married to John Harris.

Elizabeth Smith, wife of Dr. William Van Duyn.

Catharine Smith was married to Hamilton Murray.

Rhoda Smith became the wife of Nial R. Nye.

Amy Smith was Mrs. Dr. Abel Phelps.

James Smith, Jr., married Sally Hubbell, sister of Capt. Jesse Hubbell. He died August 8th, 1844, aged 61 years 6 months.

Mrs. Smith died April 20th, 1861, aged 61 years.

Esquire John Smith married Betsy Monroe and lived on the old homestead. He died in 1872. They had a numerous family of sons and daughters.

The daughters were: Polly, Mrs. Stone, of Washington county, O.; Betsy, Mrs. Russell; Catharine, Mrs. Fulsom; Jane, Mrs. Erastus Stow.

Mr. Stow died in 1842, and Mrs. Stow died in 1870.

The Stow family: Eliza, married Dr. Augustus Watkins.

Euretta Stow was married to Franklin Knight, of Chester, Meigs county.

Mary Stow was married to David R. Jacobs, and resided in Pomeroy.

James Smith Stow, born July, 1806, went to Washington county, and died there in 1895, aged 89 years 1 month.

John Stow went to California—to Mississippi with a boat of produce, and died in the south among strangers.

Erastus Stow married Lucretia Whaley and lived on the old Stow farm. He was a soldier in the Civil War until its close, when he returned home and died. Mrs. Stow died December 18th, 1895. They had a family.

Luke Brine moved with his family from Rutland, Vermont, to Leading Creek in 1805. He bought a farm near New Lima. He sold his farm to Horace Holt in 1824 or '25, and moved to Marion county, O. His children were three sons and three daughters.

Jonathan Brine, a son, married Elizabeth Bobo, of Athens county, O. He was an ordained minister of the Christian Church. They had a numerous family. One daughter, Eliza H., was married to B. F. Stivers, a blacksmith, who lived in Pomeroy.

Lumon Brine was born in Rutland, O., in 1806. He married Lena Sylvester, and had a family of children. Lumon Brine died April 16th, 1879. His widow lived on the home farm with her son-in-law, Harvey Stansbury, until her death in October, 1887, aged 81 years, 7 months, 18 days.

Almon Brine lived in Indiana, and died there.

Betsy Brine married William Gaston.

Sophia Brine was the wife of William Larue.

Semela Brine was the first wife of John Gaston.

Thomas Gaston was a native of New England, and served seven years in the Revolutionary Army. He moved with his family to the State of New York, and afterwards, induced by liberal grants of land, emigrated to Canada. But on account of conscription measures by the British government and the unfriendly feeling existing between that government and the United States, he disposed of his property there at a sacrifice, and with others in like condition left Canada, and came to Ohio, landing at Silver run, Gallia county, in 1807. He was a millwright, and moved to the Higley Mills. Later he bought a farm near New Lima, where he spent his remaining days. He was a member of the Regular Baptist Church, and preached occasionally. Mr. Gaston and his wife had a large family. He was a man highly esteemed by all who knew him. He died in 1823 and was buried in the Miles graveyard.

Mrs. Gaston died some years after, while with some relatives in Indiana. Their children were:

Jared Gaston, married Sally Stivers.

Anson Gaston married Lucretia Holt.

William Gaston married Betsy Brine.

Jonathan Gaston's wife was Selusia Morton.

John Gaston was married twice; his first wife was Semelia Brine, and for his second wife Lydia Larue, who was born March 6th, 1806.

Her parents were Jacob Larue and Sally Gardner, who were married in the Block House at Marietta four or five years before Ohio became a State. Her grandfather, Abraham Larue, was a French Huguenot. Mrs. Lydia Gaston was married a second time, to Thomas Wood, who died in 1876, while Mrs. Wood continued to live in the old Gaston homestead until her death in 1893.

James Gaston married Mary Woodworth, in Canada.

Thomas Gaston, second, died when quite a young man.

Elijah Gaston married Samantha Woodworth and emigrated to the West. The daughters were: Hannah, Mrs. Joseph Richardson; Polly, Mrs. Joseph Skinner. All are dead, 1893. Roena.

Frederic Hysell was a soldier of the Revolution and came from eastern Virginia to Ohio in 1805, to the lower part of Gallia county, but afterwards moved to Salisbury township, in what is known now as Middleport. He married Nancy Smith, and they had sons and daughters. Mr. Hysell died at a good old age, and his wife died in 1823.

Their children: Edward Hysell lived on a farm in Salisbury township. Catharine, Mrs. Jason Thomas, settled in lower Rutland township. Elizabeth, Mrs. George Hoppes, lived in Salisbury, near Bradbury. Margaret, Mrs. Anthony Hysell, lived on Thomas fork. Francis Hysell married Nancy Dodson and lived on a farm on Hysell run. Smith

Hysell married Elizabeth Hunter and lived in Salisbury township. Owen Hysell married Sophia Archer and lived in Salisbury township. John C. Hysell moved into Rutland township on a farm on Hysell run. Mr. John C. Hysell enjoyed the confidence of his fellow citizens. He was township clerk seven years and served as justice of the peace for Salisbury eight years and for Rutland twelve years—twenty years entitled him to be 'Squire Hysell always. He was county commissioner one term, when the court house was built at Pomeroy, and superintended the same. He belonged to the Christian church in Rutland, and was an active, useful elder for many years. His wife was Miss Jane Bailey.

Nancy Hysell, a daughter of Frederic Hysell, was married to Enoch Murray and lived on Thomas Fork. She died in 1892 or 1893.

James B. Hysell, of Middleport, was a son of John C. Hysell, a good citizen, held several responsible offices, was mayor of Middleport, trustee of the Meigs County Children's Home, and held other positions of honor. He died in 1906.

Joshua Johnson (supposed to be from Portugal) came to Ohio in very early times, and bought a valuable tract of land in what is now Scipio township, and included the land where Harrisonville is located. He was married twice, and of the first marriage he had one son and two daughters. His second wife was a sister-in-law of Mr. Trickler, a wealthy farmer of Gallia county. This marriage was favored by two sons and one daughter. The eldest son, Isaac, went to a place near Cincinnati, Ohio; and the sisters, Kate, Mrs. McHenry, and Milly, Mrs. John Ervin. The second son, David, married Mrs. Paton, and after a few years moved to Missouri. James married his brother Isaac's widow and lived where his father did. The third daughter, Polly Johnson, was a maiden lady, taught school in Ohio and in Missouri. She was a much respected and enterprising woman, and during the excitement caused by the discovery of gold in California she emigrated with some relatives from Missouri to the gold fields, where it is supposed that she died.

Leonard Hedrick was born in North Carolina May 14th, 1784, and came to Marietta, Ohio, in 1800, and went on the first ship commanded by Captain James Merrill as a cabin boy to the ocean. When he returned, he married Elizabeth Loucks, of Gallia county, but settled on his own farm in Scipio township. Mr. Hedrick was a soldier in the War of 1812 and served under Colonel Robert Safford in the Northwest campaign. Mrs. Hedrick was born February 3rd, 1786. Their children were: Margaret, born February 2nd, 1810, married ——— Camp, who died in a few years after the marriage; she died in Rutland, December 14th, 1891, aged eighty-one years, ten months. Mary, born December 15th, 1811, married Stillman C. Larkin, November 21st, 1837, and died in the Larkin homestead, May 30th, 1904, aged ninety-two years, five months, fifteen days. Catharine, born September 25th, 1816, married James Misner, who died many years ago. Mrs. Misner has lived in Point Pleasant, W. Va. Sally, born October 17th, 1818, married David Forrest and lived in Scipio township. William, the only son, June 29th, 1824, lives on a part of his father's farm. Malinda, daughter of Mrs. Camp, moved to West Virginia, married W. Starkey. Mr. Lemuel Hedrick died March 29th, 1861, aged seventy-six years and ten months. Mrs. Hedrick died March 4th, 1870, aged eighty-four years and one month.

Mr. Hedrick was a good citizen, reliable and industrious.

Aaron Holt came originally from near Hartford, Conn., but after the Revolutionary War was induced, like many others, to go to Canada for cheap lands, but became dissatisfied and removed with his family to Rutland, Ohio, in 1807. His son, Horace Holt, was born October 7th, 1798, in Connecticut, near

Hartford. He married Malinda Bellows, daughter of Benjamin Bellows, of Rutland, Ohio, January 1st, 1824. They had a family of five children: Columbus B. Holt, Nial N., Electa, Mrs. John Stansbury, died many years ago; John B. Holt and Lovina, Mrs. S. D. Webb. Horace Holt died in Rutland, Ohio, March 6th, 1885, aged eighty-six years. Mrs. Holt, neé Malinda Bellows, was born September 4th, 1805, in Belpre, Ohio, and came with her father's family to Rutland in 1822. She died May 20th, 1893, aged eighty-seven years, six months and twenty-five days. She was much respected for her benevolence and Christian character.

William Bellows, a son of Benjamin Bellows, was born June 1st, 1816, and married Amelia Flynn, daughter of Thomas Flynn and wife, who were early settlers of Lebanon township. They had a large family. He was killed in a runaway of frightened horses August 18th, 1893, aged seventy-seven years two months. Mrs. Amelia Bellows was born September, 1817, and died December 16th, 1895, aged seventy-eight years three months. They had lived a married life of fifty-six years, respected by their neighbors and the community.

The manufacture of weavers reeds was commenced and carried on by Horace Holt in Rutland township, Ohio, from 1823 until his death, March 1st, 1885. The history of this industry, as well as that of the man who prosecuted the business, is worth a page of careful record. When a young man, Mr. Holt went to the Wabash country, in Indiana, and was taken sick, and while convalescent he found an old weaver's reed, which he unraveled to find how it was constructed. This led to a knowledge of the canes from which the splits were made. Returning to Rutland, he began in earnest to make weavers reeds. He obtained the canes from Mississippi by sending men down the river to cut canes, convey them to the river and to purchase boats to load with these and bring them to Leading creek, a tedious and expensive enterprise.

Mr. Holt, seeing the need of a proper machine for making the splits, made such a one, which worked well, and went to Washington, D. C., and obtained a patent. He went in a two-horse wagon, laden with reeds to sell on the way as well as to take his model for a patent, to the city of Washington. In 1831 he began to manufacture reeds on a large scale. The sale of reeds had been by peddlers in wagons, traveling over the country and taking store goods in return for the reeds. That began the stores for the firm. Mr. Holt employed his brother-in-law, John Rightmire, who was a blacksmith, to make his machines, so that he secured complete control of the weavers reeds manufacture. It is claimed that at one period of time his was the only reed factory in the United States or Canada. His books show that he had made 300,000 reeds, that brought about $200,000. Mr. Holt paid good wages and treated his employes fairly, and his business was a great advantage to the community, as it furnished remunerative employment for many young women who otherwise could have earned but little. Mr. Holt was of commanding figure and had a giant's strength. He engaged in other kinds of business besides the making of reeds. In a partnership with Mr. Clem. Church they built the first steam gristmill in Rutland township, and he owned and brought into the township the first thrashing machine. Before the Civil War he was an abolitionist, and his place was a station on the "underground railroad." A member of the Universalist Church, he was exemplary in speech and honorable in business habits, never using intoxicating liquors or tobacco, and in his last years he was a prohibitionist. He sold the reed manufacturing business to his son, John B. Holt.

Meigs county is the richer for having had such an enterprising citizen.

Peter Lalance came from France with his widowed mother and sister about 1788 to Marietta, Ohio, and lived in the stockade at Harmar. The sister was married to Robert Warth, who was killed by the Indians just outside of the fort, leaving a wife and one child, Robert Warth, Jr. Peter Lalance was a comrade of the Warth brothers on their voyages down the Ohio river to Gallipolis, or French Town, as the Americans called it. The Warths, George and John, were carrying United States mail in their canoes, and young Lalance was a companion. The company had to stop over night each trip, not being able to go all of the distance in one day, and the place for stopping was at Jacob Roush's, near or at Graham's Station, Va. Mr. Roush owned a farm and slaves. He had a family and, as the story goes, a handsome daughter, whose beauty captivated the heart of Peter Lalance, but he kept his secret until meeting his mother, when he described mam'selle to her. "She's very pretty," summed up his account. "Bring her here," said his mother; "I can teach her." So, with such permission, he asked Mr. Roush if he might woo his daughter. "If she is willing," was the father's consent, for up to this time the ardent lover had not ventured to propose to the girl. Matters were arranged for mam'selle to go to Marietta on the "mail boat," a trusty colored man to accompany the young woman for her protection. Madame Lalance received her graciously, and afterwards she was married at her father's house to Peter Lalance. He located a farm below Bowman's run, in Ohio, and reared a large family. Communicated by Mrs. Cynthia Philson, of Racine, Ohio.

Mrs. Mary Lasher was a daughter of Aaron Holt, and his wife, Elizabeth Holt, and was born in 1803, and came with her parents to Rutland in 1807. She was married to Charles Chase in 1823, and had a family of nine children, all of whom she reared to be respectable and useful citizens. Dr. Owen Chase, of the West, and Dr. Lyman Chase, of Albany, were her sons. After the death of Mr. Chase, she married Mr. John V. Lasher, of Rutland, with whom she lived in social and religious harmony until his death, which preceded her own about two and one-half months.

John V. Lasher was born August 9th, 1799, in Dutchess county, New York, and married Catharine Martin, October 24th, 1820. In 1825 they moved to Sullivan county, New York. In 1835, in company with his brother-in-law, Frederic Tuckerman, they came to Ohio and settled on a farm in Rutland township. They had a large family of nine children: William V., Charles, George V., Margaret, Mrs. Green; Mary, Mrs. Tuckerman; Beattie, Mrs. Stansbury; Carrie, Mrs. Brown. Mrs. Catharine Lasher died in 1864. Afterwards Mr. Lasher married Mrs. Chase, widow of Charles Chase. Mr. Lasher seems to have favored all religious and political reforms. First a Whig; then one of two or three who voted for Birney, the Liberty Party man, and in his last years for the Prohibition Party. He died in 1864.

STOW AND THE WOLVES.

An incident related by Mrs. Eliza Watkins, neé Stow: Mr. Erastus Stow, at an early period, when a young man, was employed by Captain James Merrill to stay with his family in Salem while he (Captain Merrill) was taking a vessel from Marietta to the ocean. Young Stow started with ten bushels of corn to get ground on the Ohio or Muskingum. After being gone a week, he returned to the mouth of Leading creek. He then took a bushel of meal and started for home and walked as far as Mr. John Miles, where he stopped and borrowed a horse and proceeded on his way. Before he reached home it became dark, and wolves began to howl and made an attack on him. Both he and the horse were frightened. He threw off the bag of meal, put his feet on the horse's flanks and his arms around the animal's neck and made all speed to his home. When he arrived, Mrs. Merrill and the family came out, having heard the noise, and with firebrands drove the wolves away. The next day they found the sack of meal, which had been torn open, but the contents not destroyed.

Such incidents did not often occur, and the people did not seem to apprehend much danger. Women and children often went through the woods, hunting servis berries and grapes, or frequently to hunt the cows, that would often stray from home, and were seldom molested.

A BRAVE BOY.

An account given by Mrs. Sarah Torrence of an incident worthy of note was read at the pioneer meeting in August, 1879, by Mr. A. Gardner. Mrs. Torrence was a daughter of Mr. John Knight, who came to Meigs county in 1818. A Mr. John Harris, who lived in Bedford township, got Mr. Knight's son Daniel, a lad of only eleven years, to stay with Mrs. Harris while he made a trip to New Orleans. There were few families in Bedford township, and it was very lonesome for the young wife in the small cabin in the woods, where the wolves were heard nightly. So Mrs. Harris concluded to go down to her father's, Mr. John Smith, above the mouth of Leading creek, and a son of Mr. Bissell, who was younger than Daniel, was engaged to stay and care for the stock. One night early in March, as these boys were getting in a log to build a fire in the morning, young Knight slipped, and the log fell on him, breaking his thigh bone about the middle. Daniel told the Bissel boy to pull their straw bed down before the fire. Then he lay flat on his back, with one hand on each side and the fingers of each hand thrust through the cracks of the puncheon floor, directing the other boy to pull at his foot while he held on to the floor, until they actually set the bone in its place. He had buckskin pants and took some buckskin thongs and tied above and below the break, the pants serving as splints. Fortunately, Major Higley had gone out that day to look after some stock, and called in to see how the boys were doing and to spend the night with them, and this was the plight in which he found them. They had corn bread of their own baking and venison. Mr. Higley examined the boy's leg and found that it was broken, and he then mounted his horse and rode to Mr. Knight's, the father of the boy, at Middleport, who immediately started to his son in the wilderness, going by way of Chester for Dr. Robinson to accompany him. They knew the path as far as Bissell's, but no farther. They arrived there to find that Mr. Bissell was away from home, but Mrs. Bissell got out of bed at midnight, had her horse saddled, and piloted these two men through the dense forest to where the suffering boy lay, leaving her own little one asleep at home, and stayed with the boy until Mr. Knight returned and brought his wife and provisions. Mrs. Knight had to stay twenty-one days before they could take the boy home. Those were pioneer times.

PROCEEDINGS OF THE FIRST COUNTY COURT OF COMMON PLEAS FOR MEIGS COUNTY, STATE OF OHIO, ss.:

April Term, in the Year 1819.

Be it remembered, That at a term of Court of Common Pleas for the county of Meigs, begun and held at the temporary seat of justice: Present, Hon. Ezra Osborn, president, judge of the Eighth Judicial Circuit of the Court of Common Pleas for the State of Ohio; and Horatio Strong, Fuller Elliot and James E. Phelps, Esqs., associate judges of the Court of Common Pleas for Meigs county, who produced their several commissions under the great seal of the State of Ohio, which were read in open court.

Robert C. Barton was appointed clerk pro tem. of the said court in complying with the requisitions of the law. Samuel

F. Vinton was appointed prosecuting attorney for the present and succeeding terms.

The court then adjourned until tomorrow at 9 o'clock.

EZRA OSBORN.

Second Day.—The court met pursuant to adjournment. Present: The same judges as of yesterday. The clerk, on motion, produced a bond as sureties for the faithful discharge of his duties. The same was approved, and he was duly sworn into office, and the senior associate was directed to deliver the said bond to the county treasurer.

On motion, it was ordered that license be renewed to James E. Phelps to keep a house of entertainment at his new dwelling house on his complying with the requisitions of the law. A notice was duly served on James E. Phelps and Fuller Elliot, Esqs., associates of the court, by Horatio Strong, senior associate, to meet at the temporary seat of justice on the twelfth day of April, instant, for the purpose of appointing a recorder of the county, according to law. Ordered by the court that the clerk within twenty days give notice to the trustees of each township that they make a selection of grand and petit jurors, and that they return to him thereof to him in twenty days thereafter. And he is required to have them subpoenaed to attend in their respective capacities as jurors at this place on the first day of next term, by the sheriff. On motion, ordered that licenses be granted to George Russell for a ferry across Leading creek where he now keeps it on his complying with the regulations of the law.

On motion, ordered that license be granted to Elisha Rathburn, of Rutland, to solemnize the bonds of matrimony. On the application of James H. Hayman and Alexander Miller for the appointment of county surveyor, the court was equally divided and the application laid over until the next term.

Ordered by the court that the clerk pro tem. use his private seal for all processes issuing from court until a county seal shall be provided. The court adjourned until half-past 1 o'clock P. M. The court met pursuant to adjournment. Present: Horatio Strong, Fuller Elliot, James E. Phelps, Esqs., associate judges. On petition of Thomas Ridding, of Sutton, for a license to keep a house of entertainment at his dwelling house, ordered that the clerk give him a license on his complying with the requisitions of the law. The minutes being read and approved by the court and adjourned without day.

HORATIO STRONG.

April 12th, 1819.

Pursuant to request, the associate judges assembled at the temporary seat of justice. Present: Horatio Strong, Fuller Elliot and James E. Phelps, Esqs., associate judges.

Robert E. Barton was appointed recorder of Meigs county, and on producing his bond was duly sworn into office by the senior associate judge, the bond having been approved. The oath of office was administered as follows: I, Robert C. Barton, do solemnly swear that I will faithfully and impartially discharge the duties of recorder of Meigs county according to the best of my abilities and understanding. Robert C. Barton.

Subscribed April 12th, 1819. The oath to support the Constitution of the United States and the State of Ohio being also administered, the associates adjourned.

HORATIO STRONG.

State of Ohio, Meigs County, ss.
July Term, 1819.

Be it remembered, That on Monday, the nineteenth day of July, 1819, the Court of Common Pleas in said county, at the meeting house in the township of Salisbury—present, the Hon. Ezra Osborn, president judge; Horatio Strong, Fuller Elliot and James E. Phelps, associate judges—the venire for grand jurors was returned and the following jurors empaneled, to-wit: Foreman, Daniel Rathburn; David Lindsey,

Adam Harpold, Jesse Worthing, Joel Smith, Silas Knight, James Shields, Jr., George Roush, Jas. Gibson, Calvin Marvin, John H. Sayre, Alvin Ogden, Joseph Hoit; Major Reed, talisman.

Then follows the licensing of different men for various purposes, the trial of persons for various offenses, consisting largely of "fist-i-cuffs," and probate business is omitted.

State of Ohio, Meigs County, ss.
November Term, A. D. 1819.

Be it remembered, That on Monday, the twenty-second day of November, in the year of our Lord, eighteen hundred and nineteen, the Court of Common Pleas met at the meeting house in Salisbury township. Present: The Hon. Ezra Osborn, president judge, and James E. Phelps and Fuller Elliot, associate judges, this, the last court for the first year in Meigs county, 1819.

Review of proceedings by S. C. Larkin.

The design of the following resumè is to elucidate facts that relate to the history of Meigs county, but are not generally understood.

By a law of Congress, Section 29 in every township of six miles square in the Ohio Company's purchase should be reserved for ministerial purposes. The land upon which this meeting house stood belonged to Salisbury township, and the Courts of Common Pleas were held in it for two years, when, unfortunately, it was burned down. Mr. Levi Stedman, of Chester, invited the judges to hold court in his house. When the second set of commissioners met, they went where the court was held, and decided to locate the county seat, as Mr. Levi Stedman offered to make a good deed of land, enough to lay out a town. The offer was accepted. The county seat was located there, the town laid out and named Chester. The question was asked why the county seat was not located at

Middleport? Mr. Benjamin Smith and his wife Alma had agreed to donate as a gift the land for a town and to secure it by a good title deed. Smith had given a bond for $5000, with his brother, John Smith, and Samuel Everett as sureties, but it has been stated that upon reconsidering the matter, Mrs. Smith refused to acknowledge the deed, which she had a right to do, according to the law of Ohio. The commissioner did not bring suit against the sureties, as John Smith lived on his father's farm, and Samuel Everett was a young man not owning any real estate. The judges claimed that nothing could be realized more than cost of suit, and they should not be blamed for not ordering or permitting the commissioner, Eli Sigler, from commencing suit. S. C. L.

EXTRACTS FROM REPORTS OF THE PROCEEDINGS OF THE FIRST COMMISSIONERS OF MEIGS COUNTY, STATE OF OHIO, APRIL 30th, 1819.

The commissioners of said county met this day, to-wit, Levi Stedman and William Alexander, who, after being duly sworn by Archibald Murray, a justice of the peace for the county aforesaid, and lodging a certificate thereof in the office of the Court of Common Pleas for the said county, proceeded to business.

Benjamin Stout, duly elected sheriff of said county, presented a bond, of which the following is a copy, which was approved and delivered to the county treasurer:

Know all men by these presents: That I, Benjamin Stout, as principal, and Levi Stedman and Philip Jones, as sureties, all of the county of Meigs and State of Ohio, are held and firmly bound to Levi Stedman, William Alexander and Elijah Runner, commissioners of the county aforesaid, and to their successors in office in the full and just sum of four thousand dollars, current money of Ohio, for which sum well and truly to be paid, we bind ourselves, our heirs, executors and administrators firmly by these presents. Signed and sealed this thirteenth day of our Lord, one thousand eight hundred and nineteen.

The condition of the above obligation is such, that, whereas the above bounden Benjamin Stout was duly elected sheriff of the county aforesaid, on the fifth day of April, inst., and was also duly proclaimed as such on the twelfth day of April, to serve until the annual election in October next. Now, therefore, if the said Benjamin Stout shall well and truly perform all the duties of sheriff of the county aforesaid and account for and pay over all the moneys by him collected according to law, then this obligation will be null and void; otherwise remain in full force and virtue.

[Seal] Benjamin Stout.
[Seal] Levi Stedman.
[Seal] Philip Jones.

Signed, sealed and delivered in presence of Robert C. Barton.

Philip Jones, of Salisbury, was appointed county treasurer to serve until the annual meeting in June next, and having produced bond for the faithful discharge of his duties the same was approved. Robert C. Barton was appointed clerk (pro tem).

Resolved, That the tavern of James E. Phelps, of Salisbury, and that of Thomas Redding, of Sutton, pay six dollars each for a license for one year ensuing. And that George Russell pay two dollars for a renewal of license to keep a ferry over Leading creek where he now keeps it.

June 7th, 1819. Commissioners met this day.

Present: Levi Stedman, William Alexander and Elijah Runner. The last named was duly qualified by William Alexander, a justice of the peace, and a certificate thereof lodged with the clerk of Common Pleas Court. Benjamin Stout, of Orange township, was appointed collector of the county tax for the year 1819, and Philip Jones was appointed county treasurer for one year from this date, and having produced a bond for the faithful performance of his duties in office, the same was approved.

Resolved, That six sections formerly attached to the township of Morgan, and which are within the county of Meigs, be, and the same are hereby attached to the township of Salem.

Resolved, That the three sections lately belonging to Cheshire township and numbered 24, 30 and 36, being within the county of Meigs, be and the same are hereby attached to the township of Rutland. And that the three sections lately belonging to the township of Cheshire and numbered 6, 12 and 18, being in the county of Meigs, be and the same are hereby attached to Salisbury township.

Resolved, That the original surveyed Township No. 9, in Range 13, be and the same is hereby attached to the township of Orange.

Rates of ferriage across the Ohio river that persons licensed to ferry are entitled to demand, viz: Each foot man, 10 cents; for one man and horse, 20 cents; for a loaded wagon and team, 100 cents; for any other four-wheeled carriage, 75 cents; for a loaded cart and team, 50 cents; for an empty wagon and team, 37½ cents; for an empty cart or sled or sleigh and team, 18¾ cents; for every horse, mare, mule or ass or head of neat cattle, 5 cents; for every sheep or hog, 3 cents.

Rates of ferriage across Leading creek: For each foot man, 6¼ cents; for a man and horse, 12½ cents; for a loaded wagon and team, 50 cents; for any other four-wheeled carriage, 37½ cents; for loaded cart, 25 cents; for an empty cart and team, sled or sleigh and team, 18¾ cents; for every horse, mare, mule, ass or head of meat cattle, 5 cents; for every hog or sheep, 3 cents.

Resolved, That ten dollars be allowed to the clerk of the Court of Common Pleas for services not otherwise provided for, and one dollar for opening the poll books from April 5th to June 7th, 1819. And that one dollar and sixty-seven cents be allowed to Benjamin Stout, Esq., sheriff of said county, for similar services.

Resolved, That there be allowed to the clerk of the Court of Common Pleas for the ensuing year the sum of fifty dollars in full for all services wherein the State may fail in prosecution, the same to be paid quarterly.

Resolved, That Robert C. Barton is appointed clerk of the court for the ensuing year.

Resolved, That there be allowed to the sheriff of the Court of Common Pleas for the ensuing year the sum of forty dollars in full for services wherein the State may fail in prosecutions which may be commenced, and that the sum of three dollars be allowed for opening and certifying poll books, the same to be paid quarterly.

Resolved, That all persons required by law to bring returns to the office of the county commissioners or clerk of the Court of Common Pleas be allowed 5 cents per mile for travel—the same for commissioners—and $2.25 cents per day for services.

Proceedings approved by the Court of Common Pleas, July 24th, 1819.

The board adjourned until the twenty-first of July, 1819.

An application was made this day to divide the township of Orange.

Resolved, That said township of Orange be divided as follows: Beginning on the Ohio river at the southeast corner of Section 29, Township 3, Range 11, west to the northwest corner of Section No. 5, Township 3, Range 12; thence north to the county line; thence east with said line to the Ohio river; thence with the meanderings of said river to the place of beginning; and that the name of the township be Olive.

Then follows a detailed account of expenses, much of which had to be paid in county orders.

December 6th, 1819. At a meeting of commissioners, present were Samuel Downing and Philip Jones, this being the first meeting of the commissioners since the October election of 1819.

They proceeded to draw lots agreeable to law, Robert C. Barton being authorized to draw for William Alexander in case he was not present. In drawing of lots, it appeared that William Alexander was to serve one year, Philip Jones two years and Samuel Downing three years.

An act for levying tax on land, passed February 8th, 1820:

Section 2. That all lands subject to taxation shall be rated or classed as first, second and third rate, agreeably to the following rules, to-wit: In all cases where the largest proportion of a tract of land is of the best quality, it shall be denominated first rate and shall be taxed annually as such. And when the largest proportion of a tract of land is inferior to the best and superior to the worst quality, it shall be denominated second rate and shall be charged with a tax annually as such.

Section 3. Be it further enacted, That there shall be levied and paid yearly and every year on each hundred acres of land of the first rate one dollar and fifty cents.

On each hundred acres of second rate land, one dollar; and on each hundred acres of third rate land fifty cents, and in the same proportion for any greater or less number of acres.

Section 48. Be it enacted, That 25 per cent. of the net amount of taxes collected shall be paid into treasury of such county for county purposes.

On February 24th, 1824, a law was passed altering the amount of tax on the different rates of land, as follows:

First rate land, $1.25. Second rate land, 87½ cents. Third rate was 56 cents.

Section 2. Twenty per cent. of the net tax collected to be paid into the county treasury.

February 23, 1824, another act of the Legislature fixes the rates of stud horses not to exceed the rate for which he stands for the season, but on all other horses, mares, mules and asses three years old and upwards a sum not to exceed 30 cents per year. On all neat cattle three years old and upwards, 10 cents per head. On other property made taxable by this act, not to exceed one-half of 1 per cent. of the appraised value.

The reason why the substance of the tax laws has been quoted here is in order to show that in the early years of Meigs county and in former years the Legislature of Ohio always limited the amount of tax to be raised, giving the commissioners of a county no authority to go beyond such limits. Great care was taken not to allow corporations to run the people into debt, as they now do, entailing upon future generations a heavy debt, a grievous burden to be borne.

The amount of revenue for Meigs county was not sufficient to pay expenses, and orders on the county treasury became so depreciated as to bring only 50 cents on the dollar and became an article of trade. Merchants would pay in goods, 50 cents for a dollar, and sell the same in money to taxpayers, who would pay tax with it to the amount of its face. What little money was paid into the treasury was used for expenses that orders would not pay.

The method of grading land into first, second and third grades and for fixing the amount of tax for each 100 acres, according to the respective rates for state purposes, was enacted February 18th, 1804, and was continued with slight alterations up to the first years of Meigs county as heretofore mentioned, but no part of it was allowed for county purposes.

The law of levies for county purposes by assessing a tax on stock, etc., was continued at about the same rate until after Meigs county was organized, which law was enacted February 19th, 1805.

At the pioneer meeting in 1885 Mrs. Dolly Knight had a most interesting paper concerning early days about Chester, from which some extracts are taken of facts not included in the former papers. "In 1798 Peter Grow and Levi Stedman built their first cabins in what afterwards became the town of Chester, but they did not remove their families until a year later. Mrs. Grow died before the cabins were ready for occupancy, but the father, with six motherless children, came to the place of their future home. Mrs. Stedman shared with her husband all the privation of those primitive times. She, too, had a 'bear story,' for one time when Mr. Stedman was away from home she heard something disturbing the pigs in the pen and discovered a bear. She resorted to firebrands, throwing them vigorously. The bear retreated, not getting fresh pork for supper. Many families who came from Vermont and Massachusetts and located on Shade river, in and about Chester, in the first years of 1800 ought to be included in pioneer history. Thomas L. Halsey, 1792, bought land of the Ohio Company's purchase; Jacob and Joel Cowdery in 1807 and 1808, and the Branch, the Rice and Walker families and others. Those families from the New England states brought their ideas of education with them, and until they could have a common school they would work hard by day and in the evening teach their children. They succeeded in bringing up some intelligent sons and daughters. Their books were few, but well chosen and carefully read. After Meigs county was made and organized, with the county seat located at Chester, the principal lawyers to attend the sessions of Common Pleas Court were Samuel F. Vinton and Thomas Ewing."

In various communications that have been submitted to us there has been much of the same character related by Mrs. Knight, so we have taken the liberty of making extracts from her excellent paper instead of using the entire history.—S. C. L.

It is a serious fact that among the first early settlers in what is now Meigs county and who bought land, that no subsequent account of their lives or families has been obtained, an omission which at this late day it is almost impossible to supply after the lapse of nearly a century. We find in the records of deeds of Washington county and of Gallia county names of men who bought land and made homes in what is now Meigs county. Ezra and Joshua Chapman and Levi Chapman purchased land dating to 1787. Ezra and Joshua Chapman lived and died in Letart township. Henry Roush bought thirty-six acres of land in 1808 in Letart. Adam Harpold, in 1812, a farm in Letart township. Thomas Alexander, first, in 1803. After 1810, there seems to have been a steady influx of families from Virginia, Pennsylvania and New York, as well as the earlier emigrants from New England. The names of Sayre, Hall and Price are represented by a large number of people living in Meigs county.

George W. Cooper was a son of Abraham Cooper and Margaret Cooper, neé Wetzel, daughter of Lewis Wetzel, of frontier notoriety. Mr. Cooper lived in Chester several years as a salesman in Colonel David Barber's store. Moving to Middleport, he was an active member of the Meigs County Pioneer Society, being the first corresponding secretary of the same. Mr. Cooper was one of the most upright, reliable of men and universally respected. He died in Middleport, Ohio, in 1878.

Persis O. Cooper, neé Blackstone, wife of George W. Cooper, was born in Athens, Ohio, May 22nd, 1822. She was a granddaughter of Major John White. She died at New Carlisle, Ohio, July 23rd, 1894.

Major John White was born in 1758 in Pomfret, Conn., and was a soldier in the Revolutionary army. He was said to be one of the bodyguards at the execution of Major Andre, and was familiar with all the circumstances connected with the attempted betrayal of the army by Benedict Arnold. He was one of a company that landed at Marietta in 1789 and lived in the blockhouse, serving at times as an Indian scout. While here he married Priscilla Duval. After his marriage he moved to Waterford, subsequently to Athens county, until the death of his wife in 1838, when he came to his son-in-law's and daughter's, Mr. and Mrs. Samuel Fair, of Chester, Meigs county, with whom he remained until his decease, in his eighty-seventh year. He is buried in the Chester cemetery.

Samuel Ervin built a cabin near the site of what is known as the "Horton boatyard" in 1807, being the first settler of the town of Pomeroy. Amos Partlow came in 1809 and built his cabin about where the Excelsior Salt Works are situated, and that was the second house. The third cabin was erected by Frank Hughes on the ground where the court house stands, and John Mason put a cabin on Sugar run, being the fourth dwelling house in Pomeroy. Mr. Ervin vacated his house in favor of John Bailey and built another cabin at the mouth of Kerr's run; lived there in 1815, when he sold to Nathan Clark, who was therefore about the fifth settler of the town of Pomeroy. Some of the above mentioned improvements were sold to other parties. Clark sold his improvement to Robert Bailey or Randall Stivers, who afterwards sold to Major Dill. Nial Nye bought a lot of Dill and built the first store house, where he kept the first post office in Pomeroy in 1827. Mr. John Knight bought the improvement made by Mr. Ervin of a Mr. Miles, and Samuel Grant bought the Partlow improvement.

Robert Bailey, Elihu Higley, John Bailey, David Bailey, Hedgeman Hysell, Leonard Hysell and Elam Higley met at the house of Samuel Ervin and from there started to Gallipolis and volunteered under General Tupper to serve in the War of 1812.

Thomas Ervin, Robert Bailey, David Bailey and John Bailey were pioneer keelboat men, who boated salt from Kanawha to Pittsburg, the boat being owned by P. Green and Jack Allen.

The first public road cut through the woods from Gallipolis to Chester was opened by Samuel Ervin, Asahel Cooley and

Hamilton Kerr. [Note.—The date of this road is not given, but there were settlements on Leading creek and at Athens as early as at Chester, and may have been opened as early by way of these settlements from Gallipolis to Athens.] It should be borne in mind that many roads were barely marked out for horse or foot men that were never opened for teams. Mr. Thomas Matthews settled in Chester in 1798 or 1799, and he told me (Larkin) while we were in company passing over the hill on the Rutland road to Middleport that there was where he and Hamilton Kerr and some other men whose names are forgotten located a road to Shade river, crossing Leading creek where the K. & M. Railroad crosses that stream, running immediately up the point of that hill and following the ridge all the way west of Middleport and Pomeroy, but that road was never opened for teams. S. C. L.

Mr. Ervin stated that in 1814 the Ohio river was very high, so that his father, Samuel Ervin and family, were compelled to leave the cabin and take shelter in a cave, where they lived seven days and nights, in much discomfort, as it was in the month of February.

Rutland, Ohio, March 29th, 1878.

To the Teacher and Scholars of the School in Pleasant Valley:

We propose to write a few items in relation to the early history and settlement of the little spot of earth that appears to be of so much importance and which in reality is so very interesting to the inhabitants of what is now called Pleasant Valley, the lawn where now stands the seat of learning and capitol for this community, together with its surroundings up and down the vale—

When wild turkeys and deer,
 And old black bears that prowled,
Were sought by hunters here,
 Though wolves as sentries howled.

This place in those olden days was called the White Oak Flats. Now it has been three score and ten years since the first settlement was made within its borders. I will relate a few incidents. Soon after the Hon. Brewster Higley settled with his family near the mouth of the middle fork of Leading creek in the spring of 1799, and not far from the mouth of Great run, which drains the water of this little valley into the channel of that little creek, Mr. Levi Stedman had established himself on Shade river at a point where Chester now stands and had built a mill for the grinding of wheat for the settlers. It became necessary that a road should be opened between the two places. Accordingly, it was agreed that Mr. Levi Stedman and a party from Shade river and a company from Leading creek, under the direction of Mr. Brewster Higley, should meet near the place where little George Russell lived at the forks of Thomas creek. The parties having met, proceeded to mark out the road to their respective homes. The Leading creek party marked the way very near where it is now established. When they passed through a very thick wood on what is now the Stow farm and on through the low gap to a place by the west line of the McGuire land, it being in June and night had overtaken them, the darkness was intense, not a gleam of light to direct them, when one of their number thought of an expedient, which was to get into the channel of that little stream, exceedingly crooked as it was, and to follow its meanderings to the mouth, which was open ground, so they all got safely home. This occurred in 1804 or 1805.

The first settler in this valley was Abel Larkin, who moved into his cabin April 1st, 1808, on the northeast corner of Section No. 7, in Rutland township. The second settler was Joseph Richardson, a little west, in 1809, who sold to Samuel Danforth in 1811. Mr. Danforth resided there until his death in 1845. The place had been occupied by different families until now, 1878, it is owned by John F. Stevens. Richard

Cook and James McGuire came with their families from Marietta in 1813 and settled on Section No. 1. Earl P. Archer came about that time and bought land in 1814, and Elihu Higley married Nancy Cook and settled on Section No. 2 in 1816. Bereman Bailey located a farm a little north in 1827. Hazael Lathrop, who framed more buildings in this neighborhood than any other man in his time, came from New York in 1817. He married Catharine, a daughter of Billy Wright, and lived in a cabin on the eastern border of Section No. 8. He moved farther west in 1825, but after seventy years that strip of land is known as the "Lathrop Place."

Mr. Richard Cook died July 17th, 1840, aged seventy-three years. His wife, Irene Cook, neeé Hodge, died October 7th, 1839, aged seventy-three years.

About 1812 James McGuire bought a farm in Pleasant Valley. He was born in Ireland August 14th, 1777. He emigrated to Marietta and there married the Widow Murray, who had four children—William, John, Eliza and Matilda. Mrs. McGuire's maiden name was Mary Garnet. She was a sister of the mother of John Brough, the famous war Governor of Ohio. A little story was current about Esquire Brough, father of the Governor, of his queer decisions when an acting magistrate. He made the witness pay the cost of prosecution in a case of larceny. A mechanic living in Harmar and working in Marietta had a canoe to go over to his work and back for his meals. Persons troubled him by taking away his canoe when he wanted it. He therefore gave notice that he would prosecute the first one that did it. So the next day a man came along and asked where such a man had gone. He saw him take the canoe and go out of the mouth of the Muskingum. "Did you see him do that?" "Yes." Dropping his tools, he went to Esquire Brough for a warrant, and the man and the witness were soon before the court. There the witness said he did not see the man take the canoe, that he said so "for a joke." The judge figured a little and said, "I find the prisoner not guilty. So much cost for the witness to pay." Then, addressing the witness, ordered him to pay it over quick or he would send him to jail for contempt of court, so the witness forked it over.

The Original Forest of Rutland.

S. C. Larkin. Dr. Frank Parker.

Common name.	Botanical.
White Oak.	Quercus Alba.
Black, or Yellow Oak.	Quercus Touelona.
Red Oak.	Quercus Rubra.
Chestnut Oak.	Quercus Castaneo.
Swamp Oak.	Quercus Discolor.
Pin Oak.	Quercus Polastris.
Laurel-leaf Oak.	Quercus Imbricano.
Shell-bark Hickory—Small Nut.	Caya Micro-a.
Shell-bark Hickory—Large Nut.	Caya Alba.
Bitter Pignut—Soft Shell.	Caya Amara.
Black Walnut.	Fuglans Nigra.
Butternut.	Fuglans Cinerao.
Chestnut.	Castaned Visca.
White Elm.	Ulmas Americana.
Red, or Slippery Elm.	Ulma Fulva.
Sycamore.	Platuus Occidentalis.
Beach.	Fagus Peptugintalis.
Birch.	Betula Nigra.
Bass-wood, or Linn.	Filia Americana.
Cherry.	Prunus Serotiva.
Buckeye.	Aesculas Flava.
Box Elder.	Negando Acervides.
Cotton Wood.	Populus Monilifera.
Yellow Pine.	Pinus Milus.
Red Cedar.	Juniperus Virginicana.
Cucumber.	Magnolia Acuminata.
Hemlock.	Albies Canadensis.
Peppuridge, or Gum.	Agarsa Multiflora.
Persimmon.	Dios Virginiana.
Aspen.	Populus Premuloides.

Sassafras.	Sassafra Officinalis.
Honey Locust.	Gleditschia Triacanthes.
Yellow, or Black Locust.	Robinia Pendracanthus.
Mulberry.	Morus Rubra.
Sour Wood.	Oxigdendrum Arboreum.
Horn Bean, or Iron Wood.	Ostrya Virginica.
Servis Berry.	Amelanckier Canadaensis.
Sweet Pignut.	Caya Glabadendroir.
Poplar, or Tulip.	Lilliodendron Tulipifera.
White Ash.	Fraxicanus Americanus.
Blue Ash.	Fraxicanus Quadrangulata.
Crab Apple.	Pyrnes Coronarid.
Black Haw.	Vesburnem Prunifolium.
Plum.	Prunus Americana.
Papaw.	Asimena Triloba.
Red Bud.	Cercis Canadensis.
Waakoo.	Enonymas Stropurpurens.
Blue Beach.	Caspunnus Americana.
Dog Wood.	Cornus Florida.
Willow.	Salix Alba.
Witch Hazel.	Hamamillis Virginica.
Spice Bush.	Benjoin Oderiferen.
Prickly Ash.	Lanthorylum Americana.
Laurel.	Kalmia Augustifolia.
	Glabra.
Sumach.	Rhus Canadiensis.
Elder.	Sambucus Canadaensis.
Leatherwood.	Dioca Palustris.
Hazlenut.	Corylus Occidentalis.
Bladdernut.	Staphylia Trifolia.
Hackberry.	Celtis Occidentalis.
Sugar Tree.	Acer Saccharinum.
Soft Maple.	Acer Rubrum.
Blackberry.	Rubus Wilborns.
Raspberry.	Rubus Occidentalis.
Green Briar.	Amilox Rotundafolia.
Eglantine Rose.	Rosa Rubignosa.
White Hydrange.	Hydrangea Arboresceus.
Arrow Root.	Viburuma Acerifolime.
Buckberry.	Rhaninies.
Huckleberry.	Gaylussaceid Resinosa.
Blueberry.	Vaccinium Pennsylvanicum.

Wild Tea.	Ceanothis Americanus.
Frost Grape.	Vitis Cordifolia.
Hill Grape.	Vitis Aestivalis.
Bitter Sweet.	Celastrus Celastricus.
Poison Ivy.	Rhus Toxicodendron.
Virginia Creeper.	Ampelopsis Lugnesolia.
Trumpet Flower.	Tecoma Rudicaus.
Yellow Perila.	Lanthrhoriza Aperfolia.
Pea Vine.	Ipomea Prisforea.

REMARKS.

The pea vine, though small, is said to have been excellent food for buffalo and deer, and was freely devoured by the horses, cattle and sheep of the early settlers. It grew plentifully in the Rutland woods, and was much depended on as food for stock in warm weather. The wild tea is a small bush that grows on the hills. The first settlers gathered it when in bloom in June, dried it, and used it instead of tea from China, and considered it a good substitute. The wild cherry was a noble specimen of the forest trees, while it did not grow as large as some others, the poplar or oak, yet it has always been highly prized for the fine texture of its grain and bright color of its wood. It was much sought after by cabinet makers.

A few cucumber trees grew on Section 28, but have disappeared. S. C. L.

Times of the Dogwood being in full bloom as record of early or late seasons:

Years.	Months.	Days.	Years.	Months.	Days.
1840	April	14th	1870	May	3rd
1841	May	2nd	1871	April	13th
1842	April	6th	1872	May	1st
1843	May	10th	1873	May	7th
1844	April	15th	1874	May	13th
1845	April	24th	1875	May	18th
1846	April	25th	1876	May	6th
1847	May	2nd	1877	May	4th

1848	April	23rd	1878	April	18th
1849	Missed record.		1879	May	6th
1850	May	10th	1880	April	25th
1851	April	23rd	1881	May	10th
1852	May	10th	1882	May	11th
1853	April	30th	1883	May	1st
1854	May	2nd	1884	May	12th
1855	May	7th	1885	May	13th
1856	May	7th	1886	April	27th
1857	May	24th	1887	May	5th
1858	April	30th	1888	May	5th
1859	May	6th	1889	April	23rd
1860	April	23rd	1890	April	29th
1861	April	30th	1891	April	24th
1862	May	4th	1892	May	4th
1863	May	10th	1893	May	8th
1864	May	11th	1894	April	28th
1865	April	22nd	1895	May	1st
1866	April	27th	1896	April	25th
1867	May	3rd	1897	May	5th
1868	May	3rd	1898	May	2nd
1869	May	3rd			

This record of the Dogwood blossoming is because it blooms with more uniformity than any other tree, showing late or early spring, and the foregoing table has been carefully kept, year by year. S. C. L.

The name Rutland was given to the township through the influence of five of its citizens who came from Rutland, Vermont, and Rutland, Massachusetts. Their names were, viz.: John Miles, Luke Brine, Abel Larkin, Brewster Higley and Shubael Nobles. The village of Rutland was laid out in 1828, by Barzillai H. Miles and Abijah Hubbell, Jr., and the survey was made by Samuel Halliday, and the acknowledgment of the deeds for the streets before Abel Larkin, Associate Judge, August 20th, 1828. The original lots consisted of one-fourth of an acre in Section No. 14, and fractions of Nos. 1 and 7. Other lots have been added from Section No. 8 and No. 7.

MR. SAMUEL HALLIDAY,
Auditor of Meigs County Twenty-four Years.

AARON STIVERS,
Auditor of Meigs County in 1860.

SAMUEL HALLIDAY.

Mr. Samuel Halliday came from Scotland, fresh with educational honors from the University of Edinburgh, and en route to a professorship in the Ohio University at Athens, had by the difficulties of travel in a new country been impeded in his progress, and by one of those strange events in life was stranded in the little country place of Rutland, where he found his life work. He was soon engaged in teaching, and established a reputation for success in giving instruction to his pupils. Judge Ephraim Cutler sent his two sons, Manasseh and William P., to attend the "Halliday School," boarding them with the Larkins. Gen. Holcomb sent his son Anselm to be taught in the Scotchman's College at Rutland. Mr. Halliday married Miss Eliza Parker, a daughter of William Parker, an intelligent pioneer, thus locating himself as a citizen, he entered into the plans for increasing the public utilities. He surveyed and laid out the village of Rutland, and surveyed and laid out the lots in the Miles graveyard. He was influential in the erection of the two-story brick schoolhouse. When the county seat of Meigs county was located in Chester, William Weldon was the first Auditor, and after one year Mr. Samuel Halliday was elected Auditor, and served the county in that office for twenty-four successive years. He moved to Pomeroy when it was made the seat of justice, but afterwards Mr. Halliday moved to Southern Illinois, where Mrs. Eliza Halliday died. His sons were engaged in business in Cairo, having accumulated considerable wealth, and Mr. Halliday spent a few years with them.

He returned to Ohio, bought a farm in Gallia county, married a widow lady, Mrs. Braley, and passed his last days in comfortable, honorable retirement. "The memory of the just is blessed."

The brick school-house, referred to above, was used for all kinds of public assemblies, religious or political, as well as lectures on temperance or abolition. There was not a meeting house in the township, so this house was a preaching place for all denominations, when the services would not interfere with the school.

A payment of five dollars was made by the township trustees for the privilege of holding elections in this school building.

Spelling schools and singing schools met in this "town hall" and young people enjoyed the social opportunity.

There was a debating club, of considerable importance in helping young men to try their skill in oratory, or sharpen their wits by controversy. They had rules that secured to them an exclusive selection of membership.

Many intellectual contests were held there by the young men engaged in debating. The growth of minds, and the friendship of hearts, nursed in that building, will continue while life shall last with those thus associated.

THE WIND-STORM OF 1826.

The severest wind-storm ever known in Rutland from its first settlement, came on Sunday afternoon, October 29th, 1826. The school-house just mentioned suffered greatly. The upper story was swept off entirely, and the roof only was ever replaced. The strong current of this wind was not more than a quarter mile in width, showing greater strength in some places than in others in its course, which was a little south of east. It came from Salem township, but did little damage until reaching the brick house of Felix Benedict, the upper part of which was blown down. In the village of Rutland, a frame house, the residence of Mr. Beebe, was blown all to pieces, but fortunately the family had gone out of the house, and so escaped with their lives. Passing over a hill a half mile east, which was covered with heavy timber, it completely felled the standing trees. Then pitching over another hill into the valley of Hysell run, it removed all the timber except a few saplings that were not twisted off. At the base of the hill stood a log cabin, the home of Royal Hysell. There were nine persons inside when the storm began, Mr. Royal Hysell and family, and Mr. James McGuire, Sr. The house was leveled to a log or two at the bottom, but no one was hurt. Passing over Thomas Fork, near the residence of Charles Russell, the wind felled all the heavy timber on the hillside, and then passed on to the Ohio river, where the Whitlock's lived, and across the river into Virginia, and report came of its destructive path many miles into the country.

The first school in the first school-house in Salisbury township was taught by Samuel Denny, from Massachusetts, who also helped build the school-house. The school cosisted of nine scholars, viz.: James Smith, John Smith, Sarah Kerr and Christena Niswonger, these four from near the mouth of Leading creek, and five children from Judge Higley's family. This term of school was in the winter of 1801-1802. Miss Electa Higley, afterwards Mrs. Benjamin Williams, was the woman to teach in that school-house. Mr. Denny taught one year in a house that belonged to Widow Case.

Mr. Denny delivered the first oration at a celebration of the 4th of July, in 1806. He stood on a mound not far from the Case house.

Mr. Denny left Ohio in 1810, and returned to Massachusetts, where he married and died there.

Miss Fanny Smith taught school there, in 1811. She was married afterwards to Mr. Asa Maples. Probably the next school in the order of time was taught by James G. Green, a preacher, from Kentucky in 1809.

Miss Uretta Benedict had a school in a blacksmith's shop, built by Mr. Rufus Wells, but who had moved to Wilkesville. This was in 1811. The teacher was afterwards the wife of Cornelius Merrill. In 1812, Elisha Rathburn taught a school in a house belonging to Samuel Danforth that stood near the present dwelling of John F. Stevens. In 1812, a school-house was built on land now owned by Mr. George V. Lasher, and stood a few rods west of the old blacksmith shop. Miss Polly Wyatt, a lady from Athens, taught school in this neighborhood in 1812.

In 1816, a school-house was erected on land one hundred feet north of the southeast corner of Section No. 8, now owned by S. C. Larkin.

This house was built of logs, hewed or dressed on the inside as far up as the joists, with a stone chimney built on the outside, while the cracks between the logs were chinked with small pieces of wood or stone and daubed on the outside with mud. The windows for light were made by cutting out one-half of the upper side of the log at the proper height, and one-half of the log next above, on the under side, so as to match. Instead of glass, paper was fastened on, and then greased so as to admit the light. This was done on two sides of the house, and benches were made for the children to sit on, and boards laid on pins driven into the logs below the windows were for writing tables. The floor was made of boards, and loose boards were laid on joists overhead. The roof was made according to the common log-cabin style, by having eave-bearers and buttling poles to hold the long shingles in proper place. Nails were scarce and few were used in building.

The first teacher in this house was David Lindsey, who taught in the winter of 1816 and 1817. He then settled on the east branch of Thomas Fork, near the Rutland and Chester road. His successor as a teacher was Selah Barrett, who came from Vermont, bringing a young wife with him. They moved into the school-house and taught the winter school. His habit was to rise early, cut wood, make a fire, eat breakfast, and then move the household goods into the loft each morning before school hours. This was in November, 1817, and the winter 1818.

Brewster Higley, Jr., and his sister, Susan Higley, were teachers at some time in this log school-house. Mr. Samuel Halliday taught many terms in a house on the school lot, and continued to teach in different neighborhoods until the brick school house was built, where he taught until his election as Auditor of Meigs county, which office he held for twenty-four years, having been elected in 1825.

"First school-house was a small log cabin, built about 1809 on the ground now occupied by the lower graveyard in Middleport. The first teacher in that house was Jared Gaston, in 1810. The second teacher was Sally Higley, afterwards the wife of Daniel C. McNaughton, and the next term of school was taught by John Gilliland, who continued to teach about one year. The second school-house was built of hewed logs a short distance above Leading creek, on the Ministerial Section, and was designed for a meeting house, as well as a school-house. It was in this house that the first Courts of Common Pleas were held for the county of Meigs in the year 1819." Recollections, John C. Hysell, Esq., who lived with his father where the Rutland road came out to the river at the mouth of Bone Hollow, their home for eight or nine years, while he was a boy of sixteen years.

Joel Lowther was born in Loudon county, Virginia, August 4th, 1741. He was a Revolutionary soldier and drew a pension. He made his home at the house of John Stevens in Rutland, and died there November 7th, 1853. After his death, the Military Record was examined by Jesse Hubbell, then acting Justice of the Peace, who found that record made him one year older than his own account, which made him 112 years, 3 months and 3 days old, at the time of his death.

GRANT AND KNIGHT FAMILIES.

December 1st, 1817, the families of John Grant, Sr., and wife, Sarah Boltwood Grant; their sons, Samuel Grant, wife and children; John Knight and wife, neé Agnes Grant, landed at Silver run, Salisbury township, having had a long and tedious journey from Maine, which was made, first in wagons as far as Wellsburg on the upper Ohio, where a flatboat was constructed in which they floated down the river to Silver run, their destination. With them came a lad, John Pierce, whose home had been with the senior Grant for several years. Landress Grant, a bachelor brother, came also.

John Grant, Sr., died in June, 1820, and Mrs. Sarah Grant died in March, 1824. They are buried in the "Miles Cemetery," side by side.

Samuel Grant married in Maine, Hannah Davis, and they landed with a family of eight children, viz.:

Oliver Grant, married Mary Jones, daughter of Philip Jones, of Middleport, and moved to Iowa.

There was an invalid son of Samuel Grant, who lived to mature years, but died many years ago.

Royal C. Grant, the inventor and machinist of Middleport, O., married Lovina Fuller, who died many years ago.

William Grant married Esther Hobart and settled in Middleport, O. He was associated with his brothers, John and Samuel Grant, Jr., in the steam flouring mill, one of the finest mills ever built in Meigs county.

Ebenezer Tuttle Grant married Sarah Jones, daughter of Philip Jones, of Middleport. They moved to Minnesota.

Lydia Grant was married to Phineas Robinson of Chester, died many years ago, leaving two children, a son William Fenn Robinson, and the daughter Elizabeth was married to George Grow, grandson of Judge Grow.

John Grant married Mary Roup, both died many years ago.

Eliza Grant was the wife of William Wright, of Kentucky.

Cyrus Grant married Charlotte Hebard, of Athens county. He was known as Col. Grant, for many years identified with the business interests of Pomeroy. Samuel Grant, Sr., and all of his family are dead.

Mr. William Hobart came from Spencer, Tioga county, N. Y., in 1818, to Leading creek. Mrs. Hobart, neé Hugg, with two children, were with him. They had five children born in Meigs county. The older children were Isaac Hobart and Phebe, married to Mr. Hanlin, of Middleport, O. Esther Hobart became the wife of William Grant and reared a family of marked intellectual force. California, a daughter, was for years a noted teacher in the Cincinnati Conservatory of Music, and passed away in 1906, deeply mourned. Electa Grant spent some years teaching in the "New Church" Academy in Philadelphia. Julia was the wife of James Boggess, a prominent citizen of Meigs, and has been County Treasurer. William Grant, Jr., was a farmer in Great Bend, Kansas, a successful man. Lucy Grant, the youngest child, is a teacher of kindergarten schools.

There were two children of Samuel Grant and wife born after they came to Ohio, viz.: William Grant, who married Esther Hobart, and lived in Middleport. He and brother, John Grant, were enterprising and successful millers for many years in Middleport. They operated the roller process for making flour, about the first of any mill in Meigs county. Mr. William Grant was one of a company who went overland to California in 1849.

Samuel Grant, Jr., was an invalid, and died unmarried.

Belinda, the daughter, died when quite young.

Mr. Samuel Grant, Sr., operated mills in different parts of Meigs county. At the Higley Mills on Leading Creek soon after his arrival; later, he took charge of the Stedman mill on Shade river, and built, or rebuilt, the mill at Chester. He bought land and settled on his farm below Middleport, and spent the remainder of his life in the vicinity of Pomeroy and Middleport, alternately with his sons. He died in 1866 at the great age of 93 years. His wife, Mrs. Grant, lived a few years after her husband, dying "well up in the nineties," of age.

John Grant, brother of Samuel Grant, was born on April 11th, 1789, in the State of Maine. He married Mahetible Mahew, and they had two children when arriving at Silver run, Meigs county.

Thompson Grant married Cynthia McNaughton.

Franklin Grant, when a small boy, was drowned in Leading creek.

Andrew, another child, was choked to death by a grain of corn falling into his throat or windpipe.

Mary Grant was married to Elias Hutton, and moved to Delphos, Kansas.

John, Jr., married Lucinda Lellan, residing in Ottumwa, Iowa.

Sarah, first; Simpson, second; Steward Grant, living at Greeley, Iowa.

Lydia Grant, unmarried, living with her father at Greeley, Iowa.

Henry C. married Clarissa Merrill, located at Ironton, Ohio.

In 1852, John Grant, Sr., moved to Greeley, Iowa, being upwards of ninety-three years old. Mrs. John Grant died in 1864. While John Grant, Sr., lived in Rutland, O., he enjoyed the respect and confidence of all classes of the people. He was Justice of the Peace in 1826, and Township Treasurer for many years.

He died at his daughter's, Mrs. Hutton, of Delphos, Kansas, December 16th, 1889, aged 100 years, 8 months and 5 days.

This long-lived family, as the records indicate, were of Scotch descent, and known as far back as Peter Grant, who, it is supposed emigrated in colonial days and settled in Maine.

John Knight and his wife Agnes, nee Grant, came from Maine in the "Grant Company" in 1817. Their children were, viz.: Daniel, who died at the age of 18 years.

Benjamin Knight married Dolly Newell, settled in Chester, Meigs county. Calvin Knight married Jane Barton, first wife died. He then married Euretta Stowe. Sarah B. Knight was married to Samuel Torrence. Samuel Knight married Elizabeth Mitchell, a preacher of the Christian denomination, and moved to Kansas.

Louisa, the wife of Francis Chase, lived in Rutland. Both are dead.

Lydia Knight was married to John Whiteside, of Long Bottom.

Agnes Knight became Mrs. Alvin Rife, of Chester, long since dead.

Rhoda Knight was never married, but cared for both of her parents in their old age and to their death with filial devotion. She died in 1906.

Eunice Knight was Mrs. Osborn; moved to Davenport, Iowa, and died.

Olive Knight, unmarried, dead many years.

Almira, wife of Oscar Newell, of Chester, left a widow, but since dead.

Mr. John Knight moved his family six times, always in Meigs county. He opened the first coal bank on Naylor's run, Pomeroy, O. He died in Chester in 1875, in his 93d year. Mrs. Knight preceding him a year, and died aged 87 years. Pioneer sketch, by G. W. Chase, December 1st, 1882.

At the meeting of the Meigs County Pioneer Association in August, 1882, a very interesting paper was presented by Mr. Silas Jones of personal recollection of incidents related by John Warth, Esq., of events and experiences of himself and his brother, George Warth, in the early days of Indian troubles, while his father's family were living in the stockade, and where his brother, Robert Warth, was shot, killed and scalped by Indians. This paper by Mr. Silas Jones is reproduced in this history. The fact that the Warth brothers carried the first United States mail between Marietta and Gallipolis, brought out the letter of Col. David Barber, of Harmar, who was present at the reading by the secretary, Mr. George McQuigg. Before the reading of the letter, Mrs. E. L. Bicknell placed an "In Memoriam" in the secretary's hands which he read as preparatory to the correspondence with Col. Barber.

"I come today to speak of the dead, of funerals without hearse, and burials in graves hollowed out by kindly neighbors, and mourned sincerely by loving hearts. The pioneers who died were laid in plots of ground not held by any special tenure, often private burial places convenient of access to the families bereaved. In the subsequent changes of ownership of land; in the wide scattering of relatives; these places have been neglected, and graves of our ancestors have too often been lost. Allow me to call attention to a "burying ground," I use the Quaker term, as most befitting, situated on the farm of my late father, N. Bicknell, and the portion now owned by me. It is in all respects a pioneer graveyard. There have been no interments in it for forty years. Here are the graves of Mrs. Abigail Lindley, who drove the first carriage from Athens to Great Bend; Mr. Haviland Chase, from Otsego, N. Y., whose tombstone is marked with the compass and square; Mr. Isaac Laveaux Roberts, also with compass and square. He was grandfather of the well-known Capt. William Roberts, steamboatman, of Letart, O. Mr. Smith and wife, and Mrs. Smith, second, wife of John Smith, mother of Mr. Thomas Smith, and great grandmother of Prof. Thomas S. Carr, of Syracuse, O. Mr. Duncan, a Scotchman, and his wife, who came from Scotland, with the famous Nahum Ward colony. Mrs. McDaniel, of the same Scotch company, Mr. George Warth, wife and daughter. Two children of Charles and Lydia McClain, neé Roush, little ones—"Mary Jane and

Isabel." Mr. Artemas Johnson and his little daughter Margaret, and others.

Mrs. Lindley was a sister of President Lindley, first President of the Ohio University at Athens, O. I well remember his visit to his sister's grave, stopping over night at my father's house. Mr. George Warth was the real pioneer. His grave is known, but has never been marked by a stone. In regard to him I wrote to Col. David Barber, of Harmar, and received an interesting letter, which shall be read presently.

Before this letter is read, I beg to state my object in presenting these names before you. It is my wish to secure the ground where these dead are lying by a deed, in some form claiming the oversight and guardianship of the membership of the Meigs County Pioneer Society. It contains nearly one-fourth of an acre, on the bank of the Ohio river, a southeast corner lot, that might be made, with small expense, a place fair to look upon. I ask for this old pioneer, this Indian scout, George Warth, a stone for his grave. What more? The ground is grown up with brush and briars, and without a fence. In order to deed the land a survey will be necessary, and some expense will be incurred to clear it out, and enclose it with a fence. Two men are lying there with the compass and square on their headstones.

These beautiful lines,

> "My flesh shall slumber in the ground,
> Till the last trumpet's joyful sound,
> Then burst death's chain in sweet surprise,
> And in my Savior's image rise,"

are the Christian watchwords on the tombstone of Mrs. Lindley. Shall the plow of any future proprietor lengthen furrows over these graves? Will you help secure God's acre from unhallowed uses?

Col. Barber's letter was then read, he being present,:

"Harmar, April 27th, 1881.

Mrs. E. L. Bicknell:

Your favor of the 18th inst. was duly received. In reply thereto I copy from Hildreth's Pioneer History. He gives the names of families in and near Fort Harmar in the time of the Indian hostilities. Among them, George Warth and wife and two daughters and five sons. Catharine Warth, a daughter of Mr. George Warth, Sr., was married to Joseph Fletcher, a young man from New England, and settled in Gallia county. He was a surveyor of the county, and a Judge of the Court of Common Pleas. He died in 1844.

Pickett Marvin, a young man from the Eastern States, married Polly Warth, a sister of Catharine Fletcher. They settled in Gallia county, where Mr. Marvin served several years as Magistrate.

The sisters, Ruth and Sally Fleehart, who were married to George and John Warth, brothers, were noted for their skill with the rifle. It was said that Sally Fleehart could bring down a hawk upon the wing, or a squirrel from a tree top as readily as her husband, John Warth. These women had been brought up on the frontier and possessed all the intrepidity and courage of women of that class. This ends the record in Col. Barber's letter. In regard to Mr. George Warth, he was one of a party who accompanied Governor Return J. Meigs on his perilous journey down the Ohio river. He was less favored by fortune than brother John; nevertheless, services to his country should be appreciated. Silas Jones.

At the pioneer meeting of 1883, a committee was appointed to procure a suitable monument to be placed at the grave of George Warth.

Rutland, Ohio, August 14th, 1884.

The committee appointed to erect a monument to mark the resting place of George Warth beg leave to report. The amount contributed by members at the last meeting:

$8.50. Robert Combs, dime collection, $5.00. Donated outside of the Society, $16.00. Donated by L. A. Weaver, $8.00. Total	$37.50
Paid for monument	$35.00
For hauling and putting it up	2.50
	$37.50

SILAS JONES,
Chairman of Committee.

Thus are remembered the services of an Indian spy and scout, who carried the U. S. mail from Marietta to Gallipolis in a canoe, defended by his unerring rifle, and propelled by a pole in his strong hands. S. C. L.

This pioneer graveyard was surveyed and deeded to Lebanon township by Mrs. Emetine L. Bicknell, and the deed was recorded in the Recorder's office at the Court House in Pomeroy, O., in 1883. She also paid to the wife of Uriah Sayre, for her labor, and her boys, money for the cleaning of brush and briars of this same pioneer graveyard in the fall of 1882.

FLAX.

In those primitive times the raising of flax and the manufacturing of the same was an important business. It could not be exchanged for or supplied by anything else. The ground needed for cultivation had to be good, mellow land, free from weeds, and was sown broadcast. When grown and seed nearly ripe, it was pulled up by the roots by hand and spread upon the ground where it grew, and where it remained until dry. It was then bound in small bundles, and the seed pounded off with flails, after which it was taken to a meadow or pasture, and spread evenly on the grass to lie until the rain and weather had weakened the pith or inside of the stem, or rotted it sufficiently to be easily broken when dry. It was then taken up and bound ready for the brake. The brakeman would take a handful of flax and place it under the brake, and with his other hand ply the brake till all the sheaves were mashed fine. Then the ends of the handfuls were slightly combed by what was called a hatchel, and the broken stems were thrown away as useless. Then both ends were thoroughly combed, and the tow saved for use. The flax that remained after these processes was fine, smooth and glossy. The tow was carded on hand cards into rolls, or bats, and was spun on a "big wheel" like wool; but the flax was spread over a distaff and spun on a little wheel, and operated by the foot on a treadle. This thread made the warp, and the tow yarn made the filling when woven into cloth, which was called "tow and linen cloth," and was commonly worn by men for trousers in summer. The linen warp was sometimes colored with copperas, a yellow brown, and filled with woolen yarn colored with butternut bark, and was called butternut jeans, and made winter clothing. For a change, both linen chain and woolen filling were colored with indigo and made blue jeans for men and boys, coats and trousers.

Experiments were made with other material, as of buckskin, the hide of the deer, when properly tanned was a soft, pliable leather, made into gloves, mittens and moccasins, very rarely into the garments for men or boys.

Attempts were made to raise cotton, but in such small quantities, and lacking proper machinery to take the seeds out of the cotton, the effort was unsuccessful.

At a later period a few families entered into silk culture, planted white mulberry trees, and had rooms fitted for feeding the worms, but it was considered an unhealthy business, and was abandoned.

Perhaps no article of household furnishings was prized more highly than the long pendulum wall clock. The firm of Reed and Watson, of Cleveland, Ohio, made them, and sold to farmers in Rutland, on nine months' time, for twenty dollars per clock. Abel Larkin, Esq., bought one in December, 1813, and paid for it in flannel at one dollar a yard the next fall. This clock of Judge Larkin's, bought in 1813, had been in constant use, and always keeping correct time, was still running in December, 1893, after eighty years of service.

Among the few equipments of a log cabin, and a great convenience for cooking over the fire, was the crane. It was a bar of iron fastened in staples in one side of the fireplace, and movable, hung with hooks of different lengths for the use of the kettles in cooking. The teakettle, the pot with boiled dinner and the beans were easily hung over the log fire, while with a long shovel coals were drawn out from under the forestick and put on the hearth for the oven to bake the bread.

Many a family have enjoyed a supper of mush and milk, sitting around the family table with bowls for the father and mother and tin cups and iron spoons for the children. The best mush was made from the corn, grated on a tin grater, before the corn was quite hard enough to shell. This was sifted, and carefully dropped by one hand into the water boiling in the kettle over the fire, while the other hand stirred it in; it had to be stirred all the while the meal was passing from the other hand to avoid lumps, and the boiling continued during the process. The salt was put in the water first.

To make bread, mills were necessary, and the pioneers used hand-mills for crushing corn and wheat. In 1791, a floating mill was built at Marietta. It required swift water to run this mill, which was operated in the Ohio river not far from the island now known as Blannerhasset, and ground wheat for the inhabitants for many miles distant during the Indian War. Many canoe loads of grain were brought from Graham's Station, Point Pleasant and Gallipolis. After Indian hostilities had ceased, the mill broke loose from its moorings and floated down the Ohio river some sixty miles, when the chain cable got entangled in a rock and retained it. Some French settlers from Gallipolis bought it, and it was kept at Letart Falls, as the swift current there could run the mill. The first name we have been able to obtain as miller at Letart was George Burns, but it is probable he was preceded by some man whose name is not recorded.

In 1798, a floating mill was built by Col. Devol, the second one by Col. Devol and Mr. Greene, which was on the Muskingum river several miles above Marietta, which did all the grinding for the inhabitants on the Ohio and Muskingum rivers for fifty miles above and below the mill. This mill is referred to by Mr. Luther Heacox in his history of Olive township, and also by Mrs. Dolly Knight in her paper giving a history of Chester.

In 1806, a saw and grist mill was built on Leading creek by Brewster Higley, James E. Phelps and Joel Higley, Jr. Asa Daine was the millwright. The mill was known afterwards by the names of different owners, as Higley's mill, Bingham's mill and others. Several miles farther up Leading creek was the grist mill built by Samuel Denny in 1803. A saw mill was added subsequently, and this mill stood about twenty years. A log mill was built on the middle fork of Shade river by Levi Stedman about 1808, the first mill in that locality, and he used hand millstones obtained from Mr. Trueman Heacox until proper millstones could be provided.

In 1815, Thomas Rairdon built a grist mill at Long Bottom. Samuel Grant took charge of the Stedman mill at Chester in 1820, and rebuilt it, although Levi Stedman had supplanted the log mill by a frame one; still it was a water mill, needing new machinery.

Sloper's mill on Shade river farther down the stream than Chester was noted for making flour that would "raise" salt-rising bread, however dark.

The First Church in Rutland, 1824

Cross' mill on Bowman's run was far in advance of other mills in turning out good flour. This was a water mill, dating 1839.

Joseph D. Plummer and his wife Dorothy came from Newburyport, Massachusetts, to Rutland, Ohio, having spent several months at Marietta, in the spring of 1817. He bought of Eli Stedman the southwest corner of Congress Section No. 8, where he resided until his death, October 16th, 1852, aged 81 years and 3 months.

Mrs. Dorothy Plummer died December 9th, 1854, aged 79 years 3 months.

Their children were two sons and five daughters. The eldest son Ebenezer took the lead in business. He was influential in the building of the Presbyterian Church, the first church of that denomination in the township of Rutland, in 1820. Mr. Eben Plummer was a singer and led the singing in that church. After his marriage he took care of his parents for a few years, when he sold to his brother, Herriman Plummer, and moved to some Western State.

Herriman Plummer married Lucinda Stout, daughter of Benjamin Stout, who died, leaving quite a family of children, after some years. For his second wife, Mr. Plummer married Miss Rebecca Mauck, of Gallia county, and spent a few of his last years in that county. He was a man of great industry, and besides farming, he engaged in building boats, and in the salt business.

Herriman Plummer was born April 6th, 1802, and died May 31st, 1894, at the age of 92 years and 25 days.

Hannah Plummer, the oldest daughter of Joseph and Dorothy Plummer, was married to Jacob Rice, of Marietta. They had one son, Henry Rice, who lived on a part of the "old Plummer farm," and where he died in 1859, aged 36 years.

Melinda Plummer was married to John C. Bestow, of Chester, had two sons, Joseph and Henry. Mr. Bestow married for his first wife a daughter of Levi Stedman, who died leaving one son, Levi S. Bestow.

The second wife died in a few years after marriage.

Harriet Plummer was married to Robert McElhenney, of Middleport, and died November 18th, 1855.

Sarah Plummer was the wife of Lewis Nye, of Pomeroy, where he was engaged in the milling business, but after a few years moved to Illinois, where they both died.

Eliza Plummer, the youngest daughter, never married. She died November 20th, 1873, aged 26 years.

John McVey died in Salem township, February 1st, 1885, aged 94 years.

Allen Sayles came to Rutland in 1819, and died there in 1838. Mrs. Sayles died July 18th, 1851.

Mrs. Noah Smith had three daughters. Nancy, married to Capt. Jesse Hubbell, of Rutland. Jennie became Mrs. Maples, and Theresa Smith was married to Eliazer Barker, who was drowned in Leading creek in June, 1813. She afterwards married Laundres Grant.

In the fall of 1816 two brothers, Josiah and Robert Simpson, came from Penobscot, Maine, to Rutland, Ohio. Josiah bought the northwest corner of Section No. 8, Congress land, and moved his family into a house on the premises. They had a large family. Josiah Simpson, Jr., married Theresa Higley, and had two daughters—Mary, Mrs. Thomas Kirker, and Adaline, Mrs. Samuel Higley.

Josiah Simpson, Sr., died February 18th, 1837, in his seventy-seventh year, and his wife died in 1840, aged sixty-four years.

Josiah Simpson, Jr., died April 12th, 1874, and his wife Theresa died in 1862. He had married a second wife in December, 1864, a widow, Mrs. Dixon, of Albany, Athens county. Her first husband was Dr. Joseph Dixon, and they had two daughters, one of whom died unmarried. The other is Mrs. John Bradford. Mrs. Simpson died in 1890 (?).

Nathan Simpson was the second son of Josiah Simpson, Sr., born May 20th, 1812. He married Miss Liva Nye, daughter of George Nye, of Athens county, Ohio, who died June 11th, 1845, aged thirty-three years and twenty-two days. Nathan Simpson and his wife Liva had one son and two daughters. The son, G. Perry Simpson, became a lawyer and married a daughter of Mrs. Kennedy, of Salem township, and settled in Point Pleasant, W. Va., and practiced his profession while he lived. His daughter, Miss Liva N. Simpson, was proprietor and editor of the Point Pleasant Gazette some years before her marriage.

Two daughters of Nathan Simpson were Rosantha, who died young, and Mandana, who was married to Alvin Bingham, of Rutland. They lived in Middleport several years, then moved to Missouri, and afterwards they went to Ironville, near Toledo, Ohio, where two of their sons were in business. Mrs. Mandana Bingham died there in 1896.

The daughters of Josiah Simpson, Sr., were Eliza, Mrs. Ransom Harding; Nancy Simpson, became Mrs. Wheatley, of Indiana; Mary Simpson, Mrs. Simms; Betsy, the second wife of Ethan Cowdery, lived on Shade river; Ruth, Mrs. Dr. Abel Phelps, of Pomeroy, Ohio; Lydia, Mrs. Pullens; Susan Simpson, Mrs. Willis. There was one son, John Simpson, who died in early manhood.

Nathan Simpson married for his second wife Miss Nancy Hendry. He was an associate judge in Meigs county six years; later filled the office of prosecuting attorney with ability and public approval.

Robert Simpson bought the northeast corner of Congress Section No. 26 in Rutland township, 160 acres. He sold this farm in a few years and purchased a fine tract of land near

Harrisonville, in Scipio township, where he and his wife spent their remaining days. Robert Simpson, Jr., succeeded his father in the possession of the homestead. The daughters of Robert Simpson, Sr., were: Maria, Mrs. Elisha Hubbell Benedict; they moved to Kansas in 1856, and Mrs. Benedict died there. Emily Simpson, the wife of Lucius Bingham, of Rutland, Ohio; Sarah Ann Simpson was married to Jeremiah Carpenter, of Columbia township and became the mother of a distinguished family; she died in 1887, aged eighty years and four months.

Amos Carpenter, Sr., came from Virginia at an early period and settled in Rutland township. About 1818 he sold his farm there and bought a valuable tract of land in Columbia township. Mrs. Carpenter's name was McLaughlin. They spent their last days on this farm, leaving a fine estate to their children.

John Newell and family came from Massachusetts in 1816 to Fairfield county, Ohio. He had bought land in Bedford township, Meigs county, four miles from the nearest house, and did not move his family to his land until 1819, after he had cleared it and many families had settled in the neighborhood. Mr. Newell was a tanner and shoemaker.

Mr. Newell died suddenly October 14th, 1839. Mrs. Newell died in 1871. They had a large family of sons and daughters. Sally was married to Silas Burnap and was the mother of Silas Asa Burnap, captain of an Ohio battery in the Civil War. Harriet became the wife of Milton Walker, moved to Illinois; both died. Dolly Newell married Benjamin Knight, of Chester, who was a justice of the peace for twenty years; he died February 16th, 1872. Rebecca Newell married Quartus Bridgeman, of Syracuse, who died in the forties, leaving a family of six children—four sons and two daughters.

The Newell sons: Alonzo, who married Fanny Dyke and moved to Oregon, where they both died. Franklin Newell moved to the South, married and then died there. His son, Samuel Newell married Almira Knight, and their son is editor and proprietor of a newspaper in Ravenswood, W. Va. The third generation of the Newell family were all first class citizens in Meigs county. Mrs. Rebecca Bridgeman lost two sons in the war for the Union, Emory and Austin Bridgeman, who perished on that ill-fated steamboat, Sultana, at Vicksburg, Miss. Zelda Bridgeman married John Blair, superintendent of the Syracuse Coal and Salt Works, Meigs county. They are both dead.

Lonnis H. Bridgeman married Artemesia Young, of Racine. He was connected with the Syracuse Coal and Salt Company for many years and superintendent of the works after the resignation of Mr. John Blair. Mr. Lonnis H. Bridgeman has ever been an earnest and successful superintendent of the Methodist Sunday school in Syracuse and in later years superintendent of the district of the State Sunday School Union.

Quartus Bridgeman married Jessie McElroy, daughter of Captain J. C. McElroy, and occupied the homestead, his mother remaining there until her death. He is identified with the best interests of the town and a worker in the Methodist church and Sunday school.

Melinda Bridgeman died some years ago, the youngest child, unmarried.

Rev. Eli Stedman was born in Tunbridge, Vt., August 17th, 1777, and was married to Polly Gates, December 5th, 1798. She was born February 19th, 1778. They came to Ohio in 1804, locating in Belpre, Washington county, but removed to Leading creek in 1805. He was a preacher of the Free Will Baptist denomination.

Mary Stedman, daughter of Eli Stedman and wife, was born June 16th, 1805, and was married to Abner Stout, of Chester.

February 27th, 1825. Mr. Abner Stout died August 28th, 1875, and Mrs. Mary Stout died May 30th, 1882. They were both estimable people and highly respected in the community.

Auralia Stedman was a daughter of Eli Stedman and wife, and was born June 22d, 1815, in Rutland, Ohio. She was married to Mr. Branch, of Chester, who died, leaving her a widow with two children. Afterwards Mrs. Branch was married to Mr. Bartlett Paine, of Rutland. She died May 27th, 1889, aged nearly seventy-four years.

Alexander Stedman, son of Eli Stedman, was born in 1800 and died in Minnesota in 1869.

Elihu Stedman was the youngest child of Eli Stedman and wife. He married Adaline Elliott, daughter of Simeon Elliott, Esq., and a sister of Rev. Madison Elliott, at one time principal of the Chester Academy. Elihu Stedman lived in Middleport many years, but moved to Iowa. Both are dead.

Captain Jesse Hubbell was born September 25th, 1788, in Cooperstown, N. Y., founded by the father of James Fennimore Cooper, the novelist. He served an apprenticeship to the tanning business. In 1808 he came to Rutland, Ohio, where for a long series of years he followed his trade. He was a soldier in the War of 1812, serving under General W. H. Harrison, and was familiarly called Captain Hubbell on account of the years spent in military service. He was justice of the peace six years and one of the trustees of Rutland township eighteen years. He married Nancy Smith, a daughter of Noah Smith and his wife. They had two daughters, Lurinda Hubbell was the wife of Curtis Larkin, who died about 1847; Sarah Hubbell, who was married to John Easterday.

Captain Jesse Hubbell died October 17th, 1874, aged eighty-six years.

Seneca Haight was born in Washington, Dutchess county, N. Y. He came to Rutland, Ohio, in 1835. He held several offices of trust—as township clerk two years, commissioner one term and justice of the peace nine years. He had two daughters. Phebe Ann Haight was married to James Williamson, of Buffington Island; died in the eighties. Mary Haight was the wife of William Skirvin. Both are dead.

Mr. Seneca Haight died November 23rd, 1855, aged fifty-nine years.

Stephen Titus was born in Dutchess county, N. Y., June 20th, 1796, and moved to Meigs county in 1833, and was married to Margarhetta Lois Nye, daughter of Melzar Nye, of Leading creek, December 18th, 1836. He was an active, energetic citizen. He represented this county in the Legislature in 1840-41. He was president of the Meigs County Agricultural Society and was president of that society six of the first years of its organization. He died at his residence in Rutland September 13th, 1871, aged seventy-five years, universally respected and lamented. They had four children, Samuel, Phebe, Margaret and George.

Mrs. Stephen Titus was no ordinary woman. With a perfect physique, fine mental equipment, a thoroughly decided moral attitude for country and for God, she was a "perfect woman, nobly planned." She was a member of the Presbyterian Church in Rutland for seventy-seven years; also a member of the Pioneer Association of Meigs county. She died October 31st, 1907, aged ninety-two years and two months. Her home was with her son, George Titus, in the old homestead. He is quite a prominent farmer; was sheriff of the county one or two terms.

Major Samuel Titus was a soldier in the Civil War and lost an arm. Margaret died in January, 1902. Phebe, Mrs. Gleason, lives in Kansas.

Melzar Nye purchased land from Ebenezer Nye in 1809, situated below the mouth of Leading creek, but did not make a home there until 1826, when he came to Meigs county with his family. There were five daughters and one son, Melzar

Nye, Jr. The daughters: Sarah became the wife of Lewis Maguet, of Gallipolis. Margarhetta was married to Stephen Titus and lived in Meigs county. Mary Nye was married twice; first husband, Nicholas Titus, and after his death the second husband was James Brown.

Alvira Nye and Almira were twin sisters. Alvira was Mrs. Thomas Fessler and lived on the Nye farm, where Mr. Fessler died. Almira Nye was married to Mr. Gates, of Gallia county. Melzar Nye, Jr., moved to Mississippi. Prominent members of the community while in Meigs county. All are gone.

Lewis Nye entered land in 1809. Nial Nye, Sr., lived at the mouth of Kerr's run, before Meigs county was organized. He had a family of sons and daughters. The sons: Lewis, Rodolcue, Milton, Buckingham, Edward and Henry. He had a store, and a postoffice called Nyesville, of which Mr. Nye was the postmaster; a boat landing for receiving and shipping goods to Chester and other places; a sawmill that was in operation many years. Lewis Nye and Aaron Murdoch were successors of Haven & Stackpole in the steam flouring mill; later Lewis Nye moved west. Milton Nye went to a Western State. Rodolcue lived and died in Meigs county. Edward Nye died. His two sons are prosperous business men in Pomeroy.

Murrain.—One of the greatest difficulties with which the early settlers had to contend was a disease affecting cattle, and causing much loss, was known as murrain. There were two kinds; one called dry murrain was the most prevalent, in which the manifolds became fevery and dry, and stopped all natural passages. The animal would linger a few days in great distress and die.

The other form was called bloody murrain and consisted of internal hemorrhages that generally proved fatal.

Many remedies were tried with little success. The murrain gradually disappeared after 1820.

Abel Larkin was unable to raise a yoke of oxen before that time without at least one of them dying with murrain.

It is said that Daniel Rathburn lost eighteen head of cattle in one season with murrain.

William Parker came to Rutland in 1804, and built a cabin, and in 1805 moved his family from Marietta, bringing with him three yoke of oxen, and the nigh ox out of each yoke, died of murrain. Good steers were the only property commanding cash in those days. Drovers would buy them at a low rate and drive them on foot to the eastern markets. They were not bought by weight, but by the head, according to terms agreed upon by the parties.

Another singular and disagreeable disease, though not fatal, was that of slabbers in horses. They would stand, while a copious flow of saliva would issue from the mouth until puddles of water would collect at their feet. The horse would become thin in flesh, and his strength be greatly diminished. The disorder came immediately after the introduction of the white clover, and the cultivation of the grape. Many causes were assigned by different persons as the cause of the disorder, but it is uncertain if any one discovered the real source of the trouble. It continued many years and affected other kinds of stock, but gradually disappeared from the country.

HISTORY OF THE CICADA, OR SEVENTEEN-YEAR LOCUST.

After the first settlement on Leading creek, in the year 1812, the cicada made their appearance and periodically in seventeen years subsequently, as in 1812, 1829, 1846 and 1880. There seemed to be districts or locations where the locusts were seen in great numbers in these seventeen-year dates. The east and west lines between these two districts crossed the Ohio river near the mouth of Old Town creek, thence back into West Virginia at or near Racine, Ohio, and back into Ohio at Silver run, passing north of Cheshire in Gallia county and moving on to Scioto county. There is a curiosity about the line of the two districts that they continued nearly straight without regard to the crooked Ohio river. They made their first appearance from the 15th to the 20th of May, according to warmth or coolness of the season, and remained about forty-five days before they all disappeared. The males belong to the "drum corps," while the female pierces the small twigs and limbs of trees and deposits her eggs. These in due time fall upon the earth, where they remain for another period of seventeen years, to mature their growth for a few days' work in the sunshine, which seems necessary to continue the existence of their species.

These cicada were destructive to young orchards as well as other green and growing shrubs. A gentleman in Lebanon township had an orchard of choice variety of apples, and hearing of these "seventeen-year locusts" just coming into notice, turned his flock of a hundred geese into his orchard who, devouring the pests as they came up from the ground, protected and preserved his fruit trees from any damage.

When the first settlers came to Ohio they found great numbers of wild turkeys, a large bird seen in flocks in the woods, but harmless in every way. In the fall of the year men of the settlement caught them in pens built of rails from a fence near by, and generally placed on a side hill, and were about three feet high, and covered with rails. Then a low place dug at the lower side of the pen, and extending under, just large enough for a turkey to enter, would be strewed with a little shelled corn, leading into the pen where more corn would be scattered inside. The turkey eating followed the trail into the pen, and one after another all would go in. When they wanted to go out, their heads would be up, never looking down at the entrance hole. A man with a club would go in, even where the turkeys did, and kill all, or as many as he desired. The meat was fine, and frequently a very large fowl would be with the flock, so that they furnished many a good dinner for an emigrant's family. The feathers were not elastic or fluffy, though some attempts were made to use them for beds and pillows, while the wings and tail feathers were serviceable for fans and dusters.

The pheasant and quail remained here all the year, but crows and blackbirds seen in large numbers in the spring and summer, migrated in the fall. The wild pigeons passed over in vast numbers when going north or south, in the early or late season. Large flocks would sometimes tarry for a while in the fall and select a roosting place, where might be seen pigeons coming from every direction to stay all night. Men would sometimes visit those roosts at night and capture many birds, which were used for food.

The wild goose was often seen by the early settlers, on their yearly migration from the lakes and swamps of the South to the lakes and swamps of the North, fleeing the approach of cold weather in each case. They moved in large flocks, with a leader to direct their course, following in a closed-up column in a triangular shape obeying the command—a singular "honk," uttered by the leader. Southern Ohio was neutral ground, as none stopped, except a few that by weakness or some unknown reason strayed from the company.

The crane was a very large bird, not numerous, though frequently seen in warm weather.

The large owl remained in this climate during the year, and the small owl—"screech owl"—were noted for their habits of taking chickens from the roosts at night. The large owl made a peculiar "hoot" at nightfall.

The hawk was another invader of the domestic fowls, in broad daylight swooping down on a brood of young chickens and seizing one in his talons, fly away from the distracted mother hen, and only to be halted by the unerring aim of the rifle-man.

It is not certain when bees were discovered by the first emigrants. The hunters were men with strong eyes so that they could see a bee in flight, and follow it to the tree where the honey was made and stored, and chopping down the tree to secure the honey was the sweet reward of the hunters' sight and patience. Hollow gums were used for domesticating bees, and some farmers made hives with ropes of straw, sewed together so as to form a conical shaped hive for bees. Boxes were made afterwards for the same purpose, until the bee moth became so destructive that other kinds of hives were invented and patented for the protection and raising of bees.

Few of the first settlers in Rutland were hunters and did not use guns. Many of the New England men, also those from New York, were carpenters, and a few were millwrights. The first thing to use was an ax, then something to draw wood. If by oxen, a yoke with a ring in it, to which a hook in a chain lengthened out to fasten around the end of a log securely to draw to the place desired.

If horses were used, then ropes or strips of rawhide were fastened to wooden hames, which served as collars. Sleds were first used, then carts, but wagons were not in general use for many years, except by some wealthy farmers. In the house, the woman was furnished with a split brush broom. These brooms were made of a hickory pole by cutting and peeling down with a knife splits from the end to make the broom. The broom corn of later years was not known in those early days. A chest served for a table till some mill was started and boards were available, so that cross-legged tables were made and shelves placed upon pins driven into the logs. A few spiders and pots to cook with and pewter plates to eat from completed the assortment. Some families had provided themselves with home conveniences by bringing things needful from their former homesteads, but the majority of those first settlers had come from long distances, poorly equipped for traveling or for even camp life for a while. Good housewives who had brought pewter plates from "away back east" could not give them up without protest to the daughter's innovation of a lot of porcelain ware. It was claimed that the knives would all be dull if used on such plates.

Mr. Daniel Rathburn, who was a carpenter, built a frame barn without nails. He put everything together with wooden pins. This was the first frame barn erected on Leading creek.

Wheat was cut with sickles and threshed with flails, and the grain winnowed by a sheet held by two men, who employed the wind and their united force to clear the chaff from the grain.

SALT.

In giving an account of this indispensable article I will introduce an extract from the life of Griffin Green, by S. P. Hildreth. "In 1794, when salt was worth from $6 to $8 a bushel, he projected an expedition into the Indian country near the Scioto river for the discovery of the salt springs said to be worked by the savages near the present town of Jackson. At the hazard of his life and all those with him, ten or twelve in number, he succeeded in finding the saline water and boiled some of it down on the spot in their camp kettle, making about a tablespoonful of salt. While here he narrowly escaped death from the rifle of an Indian who discovered them, unobserved by the party. After peace was concluded, this warrior related the circumstance of his raising his rifle twice to fire at a tall man who had a tin cup strung to his girdle on his loins and who was known to be Mr. Green. As he might miss his object, being a long shot, and be killed himself, he desisted and hurried back to the Indian village below the present town of Chillicothe for aid. A party of twenty warriors turned out in pursuit and came on to the bank of the Ohio at Leading creek a few minutes after the whites had left it with their boat and were in the middle of the river. They were seen by the men in the boat, who felt how narrowly and providentially they had escaped."

The first settlers here got their salt from these Scioto salt works. The writer remembers hearing his father tell of taking a horse and pack saddle and going to the "Scioto Licks," as they were then called, and working a week for a sack of salt. His business was drawing salt water by means of a hand pole affixed to a sweep above. After receiving his wages, put his salt on the pack saddle and made his way home. Those salt works were under the superintendency of a state officer, and by a law passed January 24th, 1804, renters had to pay a tax of 4 cents per gallon on the capacity of the kettle used in making salt, provided always that no person or company shall under any pretense whatever be permitted to use at any time a greater number of kettles or vessels than will contain 4000 gallons, nor a less number in any one furnace than 600 gallons. After the salt works on the Kanawha were started the people here depended on Kanawha for salt, and for many years it was a place of considerable trade. Young men, on coming of age, went to Kanawha to chop wood or tend kettles when they wished to obtain a little money. It was hardly expected to get money at any other place, and salt seemed to be the medium by which trade was conducted.

Keelboats were used as a means of transportation, and shipments were made by them of salt to Marietta, Pittsburg and the lower Ohio. In order to give some knowledge of the origin and progress of the Kanawha salt business, we append a letter which appeared in the Niles Register, Baltimore, Md., in April, 1815, and we copy from the Meigs County Telegraph, April, 1884.

Kanawha Salt Works.

At the first settlement of this place there was a great "buffalo lick," as it was called, was discovered where some weak salt water oozed out of the bank of the river. After some time the inhabitants sunk hollow gums into the sand and gravel at that place, into which the water collected, but it was so weak that, although sufficient quantities might be collected, not more than two to four bushels were made in a day. After the property came into the possession of my brother, Joseph Ruffner, and myself (by divisee), we were desirous to see the effect of sinking large sycamore gums as low down as we could force them. We found great difficulty in this on account of the water coming in so rapidly. When we got down about eighteen feet below the surface of the river we discovered that our gums lodged on a solid, smooth freestone rock, and the water was but little improved as we descended. We then bored a hole in the rock about 2½ inches in diameter, the size generally used subsequently for that purpose. After penetrating the rock eighteen or twenty feet, we struck a vein of water saltier than had been attained in this place before. Our neighbors followed our example and succeeded in obtaining good salt water in the distance of 2½ miles below and four miles above us on the river. They all have to sink the gums about eighteen feet to the rock, into which they bore a hole from 100 to 200 feet deep. The rock is never perforated, though the water seeps into the holes in soft or porous places. The cost of boring was from $3 to $4 a foot. The first water that is struck in the augur hole is fresh, or an inferior quality of salt water, which is excluded by means of copper or tin tubes put down into the augur hole and secured so that none of the water that comes in above the lower end of the tube can discharge itself into the gum, which has a bottom put into it immediately upon the rock, and is secured in such a manner that no water can get into the tube except that which comes up through the tube from below. The water thus gathered in the gum rises about as high as the surface of the river at high water mark, and it requires from seventy to 100 gallons of it to make a bushel of salt. Each well produced on an average a sufficient quantity of water to make 300 bushels of salt per day. There are now established and in operation fifty-two furnaces, and more are being erected, containing from forty to sixty kettles of thirty-five gallons each, which make from 2500 to 3000 bushels of salt per day. The quantity may be increased as the demand shall justify. The wood in the course of time must become scarce or difficult to obtain, but we have stone coal that can be used for fuel, and the supply is inexhaustible. These works are situated six miles above Charleston, Kanawha Courthouse, sixty-six miles from the mouth of the river and twenty-six miles below the great falls. The river is navigable, with a gentle current, at all seasons of the year for boats drawing two feet of water, and at most seasons for boats of any size.

Your obedient, humble servant, DAVID RUFFNER.

Kanawha Salt Works, November 8th, 1814.

It appears from old account books that salt rated as high as $2 per bushel in Rutland township as late as 1820. The first salt water seen on Leading creek was a small pond of reddish water, which in dry weather cattle would visit for drink, the place being near the channel of the creek, about a quarter of a mile below the old Denny mill, in a bend of Leading creek. In 1820 several of the neighbors brought in their kettles and set them on a kind of furnace and made of that water one bushel of salt. After which a company was formed consisting of Benjamin Stout, Caleb Gardner, Thomas Shepherd and Michael Aleshire, who bored a well and erected a furnace and commenced making salt in 1822, when Benjamin Stout bought out the other parties.

In 1822 Abijah Hubbell and his son, Jabez Hubbell, and Barsley Hubbell bored a salt well above the Stout well and a furnace set for making salt in 1824.

Ruel Braley manufactured salt at his works, five miles above on Leading creek, in 1830.

The Bradford and Stedman's furnace was located about five miles below the Stout well in 1830 or 1831.

Still further down the creek Theophilus Jacobs operated a furnace for a few years with a great deal of energy.

Near the mouth of Thomas Fork Herriman Plummer bored a well and made salt in 1831.

Two other salt wells had been previously attempted in Rutland township, but failed to obtain salt water. One was bored by Joseph Giles, Sr., and the other one was by Samuel Church in 1822, which resulted in the discovery of a heavy lubricating oil, the true value of which was not understood and very little attention was paid to it.

After the Rutland furnaces began to make 200 bushels of salt per week the prices came down to 50 cents a bushel. After salt was made in large quantities along the Ohio river the works on the creek became unprofitable, and the manufacture of salt was discontinued.

In 1810 Joseph Vining and his brother, Joshua Vining, came with their families from Hartford, Conn., and settled in Rutland township, near the later residence of John B. Bradford. Timothy Vining, a son of Joseph Vining, was born in Hartford July 24th, 1805. Joseph Vining died at the age of ninety-one years, and his wife near ninety years.

Timothy Vining married Sina Jones, daughter of Charles Jones, and they had a large family—six sons and three daughters. The six sons were all soldiers for their country. Mr. Vining died at the age of eighty-seven years ten months and twenty-eight days on May 23rd, 1893.

Mrs. Sina Vining died at the age of eighty-four years.

Mrs. Jane Jones, neé McDaniel, was born and brought up in the Shenandoah valley, Virginia, until she was fifteen years old, when she came to Ohio. When twenty-four years of age she was married to Elijah Jones, of Salisbury township. They had a family of sons and daughters.

Mrs. Jones had belonged to the Christian Church for more than fifty years. She died May 29th, 1893, at the age of eighty-four years, seven months and nineteen days, and was buried in the Bradford graveyard.

Abraham Winn moved with family from New York to Canada and from there to Rutland in 1816, and bought a farm on Section 17, where he lived until his death, in 1835, at the age of sixty-four years. He left a widow and several children. Mrs. Winn died in 1860, aged eighty-six years. The children were: Joseph Winn, Sally, Mrs. Joseph Howell; Jacob Armstrong Winn, Fanny Winn, Mrs. Charles Nobles; Jonathan Winn, Lydia Winn, Mrs. Alexander Stedman; John Winn lived and died in Albany, Athens county, aged eighty-three years; William Winn went to Illinois, Nancy Winn, Mrs. Daniel Skinner.

Asahel Skinner and family moved from Maine to Rutland, Ohio, June, 1817. Mr. Skinner's first wife was Phoebe Gould, who died in September, 1817. Two of their children remained in the East; the others were: Daniel Skinner, a miller in the southeast part of Rutland; Alona, Mrs. William McKee; Joseph, Joel and William Skinner, Olive, Mrs. John Chase; Isaac Skinner, Edna, Mrs. Hiram Chase; Phebe, Mrs. William Hartinger; Asahel Skinner, David Skinner and Lucinda Skinner.

Asahel Skinner married for his second wife Jane, the daughter of Thomas Everton. Their children were: Lucinda, Mrs. Dr. Clark Rathburn; Elizabeth, Mrs. Alexander Hogue; Calvin, Marinda, Mrs. Metcalf; Samantha, Thomas, Isaac Skinner. Twenty-two children of Asahel Skinner's family.

Daniel Skinner was born in Corinth, Me., in 1801, and moved with his father, Asahel Skinner, to Rutland in May, 1817. He was constable one year and township trustee seven years. He had a numerous family. His death occurred in 1844.

Thomas Everton came from Maine in 1800 to Rutland, Ohio; bought land and made a home for his family. He was a member of the Regular Baptist Church and was familiarly known as "Deacon" Everton. His children were: Betsy, Mrs. Benjamin Richardson—first wife; Ebenezer Everton, Relief, Mrs. Edwards; Thomas Everton, Jr., Polly, Mrs. Stone; Benjamin Everton, Nancy, Mrs. Jesse W. Stevens; Sally, Mrs. Charles Richardson.

Mrs. Lucinda Pendegrass was born in Conway county, Mass., August 14th, 1793, and was married to Daniel Childs April 29th, 1813. They had a family of nine children. They came to Ohio in 1835. Mr. Childs died September 21st, 1846. Later, Mrs. Childs was married to Benjamin Richardson in 1848. He died in April, 1852. She lived a widow nearly forty years and departed this life on June 12th, 1892, aged ninety-seven years. nine months and twenty-eight days. She had led a most exemplary life, a devoted follower of her Lord. The Bible was her companion, with a remarkable memory. She read it through thirty-six times in thirty-six years. She was a member of the Baptist Church in Pomeroy at the time of her death.

John Sylvester came from Maine and located in Rutland. He married his second wife, who was a widow of Henry Filkin. They had two children, Sarah and William. John Sylvester was a son of the first wife, and John Sylvester, Jr., was a grandson of Joseph Sylvester and was noted for his great strength and his skill in wrestling.

Joseph Giles lived in Rutland and followed the blacksmith business. He married Elizabeth Townsend in September, 1822. She was born in Kennebec county, Me., March 26th, 1803, and came to Scipio, Meigs county, in 1816.

Mr. Giles died in Rutland in 1873. Mrs. Joseph Giles died in Middleport, February 18th, 1887, aged eighty-three years, ten months.

Lemuel Powell was born near Steubenville, Ohio, March 28th, 1814. He was married twice, first to Nancy Sook, and his second wife was Miss Osca Elizabeth Tingley, from near Cincinnati. Mr. Powell died January 9th, 1894, aged nearly eighty years.

Aaron Torrence was born in Allegheny county, Pa., July 5th, 1792, and came to Meigs county in 1809. He was married to Lucy Hussey in 1823. She died in 1872. They had a family of seven children, and had been married forty-nine years. Mr. Torrence married a second wife in 1873, Mrs. Rachel Horton. He was a soldier in the War of 1812 and fought the British at New Orleans. He lived a conscientious Christian life, a member of the Methodist Church, and died at Bald Knobs, July 18th, 1884, aged ninety-two years and thirteen days.

Whittemore Reed was brought from New Hampshire in 1798, a child, to Orange township, by his mother. He married Miss Stout and had a family of five sons—Darius, Aaron, Whittemore, Jr., Enos and Sardine. Darius Reed married Miss Curtis, of Washington county, and engaged in the drug business in Pomeroy. They had a family—Curtis Reed, a druggist; William Reed, banker, and Helen, the wife of Rev. Thomas Turnbull. All of these families live in Pomeroy. Darius Reed and his wife are dead. Aaron Reed married and settled in Orange, a farmer. Whittemore, Jr., married Miss Young and moved to Clermont county, a farmer. Enos Reed was married twice, first to Miss Curtis, and the second wife was Miss Ann Maria Seely. He was a druggist in Portsmouth, Ohio, but later went to farming. Sardine Reed graduated from West Point with first honors and bright prospects, married, and died in six months.

SAMUEL DOWNING.

Samuel Downing came from Waterville, Me., in 1815. He came overland to Pittsburg and then floated down the Ohio river on a raft or flatboat to Gallipolis, Ohio. In February, 1818, he removed to Scipio township, Meigs county, where he purchased land and opened a valuable farm. He was a surveyor and a justice of the peace for many years. He was an infidel in belief, until in later life he became a zealous Methodist. When Meigs county was organized, in 1819, the sheriff and commissioners were chosen in April to serve until after the general election in October of that year. Benjamin Stout, sheriff; Levi Stedman, William Alexander and Elijah Runner, commissioners. At the October election in 1819 the following men were elected for commissioners by drawing of lots. It was determined that William Alexander should serve one year, Philip Jones two years and Samuel Downing three years. Mrs. Downing was Hannah Harding before marriage. They had a numerous family—six sons and one daughter. According to their ages, they were: Samuel, Jr., George, Rodney, Franklin, Hollis, Harrison and Hannah, the youngest child. Samuel Downing, Jr., died when quite a young man. George Downing was born in Waterville, Me., April 25th, 1801.

George Downing married Harriet Chase. He was a blacksmith by trade, also a surveyor, and served many years as a justice of the peace. In 1826 an independent company of militia was organized, with Jesse Hubbell for captain, George Downing as lieutenant and Oliver Grant ensign. After seven years, the officers having served out the time of their commission, the company disbanded. He was a large, well proportioned man, of great strength. He was supposed to be the strongest man in southern Ohio. Many stories were told of remarkable feats of lifting great weights and other exhibitions of strength. He died July 12th, 1878, aged seventy-seven years and three months. Mrs. Downing died March 10th, 1890.

Rodney Downing was born in Waterville, Me., November 8th, 1802, and came with his father, Samuel Downing, to Ohio. He married Maria Black in 1825. They had two sons, Samuel, who died young, and John B. Downing, familiarly known as "Major" Downing. Mr. Downing and his wife became members of the Disciples or Christian Church in 1829, under the ministry of the Rev. James G. Mitchell. He lived in Rutland and kept a country store and dealt largely in produce, built flatboats and with a cargo of grain, fruit or hay sent them to trade on the coast of the Mississippi river in the South.

Mr. Rodney Downing built a steamboat, the Gen. Harrison, at the Stedman farm on Leading creek, in 1835, intended for the Cincinnati and New Orleans trade. He was one of the leading spirits in nearly every useful enterprise. He was clerk of Meigs county Court of Common Pleas for three terms. He removed to Middleport in 1847. Mrs. Maria Downing died October 22nd, 1870, in her sixty-fourth year. In April, 1873, Mr. Downing married for his second wife Lorinda Downing, of Harding, Lake county, Ohio. He died in Middleport, December 16th, 1886, aged eighty-four years.

Franklin Downing, third son of Samuel Downing, married Nancy Black. They were members of the Christian Church in Rutland and led consistent lives, unostentatious, industrious, highly esteemed in the community.

Hollis Downing was born in Maine June 16th, 1807. He married Phebe Smith, of Middleport, with whom he lived eighteen years, when she died. He married Jane Reed for his second wife, after which they moved to Ripley, Ohio, in 1850. He married again, Ellen Ross, his third wife. Hollis Downing died December 29th, 1889, in Ripley, Ohio, aged eighty-two years six months.

Columbia Downing was born in Maine August 23, 1809, and came with his father to Scipio township. He married Mary Gibson in 1829. Mr. Downing held many public offices, such as mayor of Middleport, magistrate, county commissioner and member of the Legislature. His first wife died, and he married Jane Smith in 1840. Columbia Downing died in Middleport, Ohio, July 25th, 1889, aged nearly eighty years. Many friends mourned at his death.

Harrison Downing, the youngest son of Samuel Downing, married Jane Graham, of Rutland. They moved to the West many years ago, and Mr. Downing died in 1892.

Hannah Downing, the only daughter and youngest child, was married to Mr. Thompson and settled in Athens county, but afterwards moved to Pontiac, Ill., where she died February 2nd, 1894, seventy-eight years of age. She was the last of the old Downing family.

Aaron Thompson was born at Racine, Ohio, in 1815. He had spent most of his life in Meigs county, but moved to Kenova, W. Va., where he lived ten years and where he died October 23rd, 1893. He was one of the first members of the Meigs County Pioneer Society. He was a communicant of the Christian Church, respected by all who knew him. He was married twice and had a numerous family. Mrs. Thompson, second, died at Kenova, W. Va., August, 1893.

Pleney Wheeler was born in Canada in 1815. She was married to William B. Pennington in New Albany, Ind., December 31st, 1835, and moved to Middleport, Ohio, in 1847. She was a member of the Methodist Episcopal Church and sustained a character of piety and good works. She died in Middleport May 29th, 1892.

Alexander Von Schritz came to Salem township in 1816, where he brought up a large family. Joseph Von Schritz was his son, born in Salem township, and married Elizabeth Sloan. They moved to Omega, Pike county, Ohio, in 1849.

The Von Schritz family were mostly daughters, married, and are scattered in the country. The father, Alexander Von Schritz, was a soldier in the War of 1812.

Joseph Townsend came from the northern part of Ohio to the mouth of Leading creek in 1812. He was a tanner by trade and made morocco leather. His children were: Maria, born March 28th, 1806, and was married to Joseph Hoyt, one of five brothers who settled in Orange township in 1813; Margaret Townsend; Sally Townsend was married to Berriman Baily in 1825, and lived in Rutland; John Townsend; Albert Townsend, and Charles Townsend, a son of Albert, a blind man, well known in Rutland, Ohio.

John McClenahan and his wife, who was a Cargill and lineal descendant of Rev. Donald Cargill, who was executed in 1684 at the cross in Edinburgh because of his religious principles, came from Palmer, Mass., in 1816 and settled in Chester, Meigs county. They had two children, Guy McClenahan, who resided in Sterling Bottom for a number of years, then removed to the great West. His sister was married to Lyman Stedman, a son of Levi Stedman, of Chester. They had three children, Lyman Stedman and Lucy, who was the first wife of J. J. White, of Portland, Ohio. Mr. Stedman died in 1828, and his widow, Samary Stedman, was married to David de Ford in 1832, who died in 1836, leaving one child. The third husband was Isaac Sherman, in 1839. They had four children. Mr. Sherman died in 1852, and the family emigrated to Kansas, finally to east Washington, where Samary McClenathan Sherman died at the age of ninety-three years. A life that began within sound of the Atlantic ocean and ended on the shores of the Pacific in 1898.

Stephen Smith was a native of New Jersey, but at an early age came to Fayette county, Pa., and later, in 1823, to Meigs county. Stephen Smith and his wife Mary had a family of fourteen children; Sally, Leighty, Annonijah, Firman, William, Josiah, John, Elizabeth, Mrs. Branch; Robert, Joseph V., James and Isaac. Two sons died in infancy.

Stephen Smith died in 1841.

Joseph V. Smith was born in Fayette county, Pa., January 24th, 1816, and came with his parents to Meigs county in 1823. He obtained his education in the schools of his native state and in Meigs county after coming here. He was a plasterer by trade, which he followed until 1854, when he was elected sheriff of Meigs county and served two terms. In 1863 he was appointed deputy provost marshal of the Fifth district of Ohio, and at the same time he held the office of United States marshal under President Lincoln. He served as deputy provost from April 1st, 1863, to April 1st, 1865, and as deputy United States marshal until 1864. During the incumbency of these offices he had many exciting experiences and narrow escapes. As provost marshal he arrested ninety-seven deserters from the United States army.

Mr. Smith married Rachel Hinckley, daughter of Abraham Hinckley, who died in 1848, leaving two daughters, Marietta and Prussia.

Mr. Joseph V. Smith married for his second wife a daughter of Ira Foster, on January 1st, 1870. He died January 14th, 1894, aged seventy-seven years, eleven months and twenty days. His daughter, Marietta, Mrs. Simms, died years since. Prussia, the second daughter, married Stephen Schilling and died in a few years.

Jesse Page came from Maine and located in Scipio township in 1816. He had a wife and three children when he came to Ohio. The children were: Edith Page, Mrs. Robinson;

Lydia, Mrs. Amos Stevens; Elizabeth, married a Mr. Page. The sons were Samuel, Sargent, Reuben and John Page.

Jesse Page died in 1834.

William Stevens was born in 1767 at Cape Ann, Mass. He came to Rutland, Ohio, in 1818, and settled on a farm near Langsville. His children were: William, Jr., Jesse W. and Rev. Amos Stevens, Sally, Mrs. Jared Gaston; Lois, Mrs. Cowdey; Betsy, Mrs. Danforth; Eunice, Mrs. Davis; Mrs. Loran Hovey was Harriet S. Rev. Amos Stevens married Lydia Page. Their children: Jesse W. Stevens, A. J. W. Stevens, Arion Lovejoy Stevens, Theresa, Mrs. Dyke; Sarah Stevens, Mrs. Dudley. Rev. Amos Stevens' second wife was Miss Anna Aleshire. Mr. William Stevens died in 1843, aged seventy-nine years.

John Bing was born in Botetourt county, Va., November 1st, 1799, and with his parents came to Gallia county, Ohio, in 1805. He came to Rutland in 1829, when he married a daughter of John Entsminger. They lived in Rutland until 1869, when they moved to Masonville, Iowa. One son, Ernest Bing, was in the Civil War.

Robert Bradford was born March 28th, 1796, in the stockade near Belpre, Washington county, Ohio. He was said to be a lineal descendant of Governor Bradford of Massachusetts. In 1822 he married Mary L. Arnold, who was born July 26th, 1798, in Rensalear county, N. Y. They came to Meigs county in 1828. Mr. Bradford sold goods in Rutland three years, and then became interested in the manufacture of salt. Subsequently retired to a farm in Salisbury township. They had a family of sons and daughters. William Wallace Bradford and John B. Bradford survived their parents.

Mr. Robert Bradford died December 3rd, 1875, aged seventy-eight years, eight months and six days. Mrs. Mary L. Bradford died July 29th, 1894, aged ninety-six years. They were good citizens and enjoyed the respect of the community.

JOSHUA GARDNER.

A synopsis of an article from the pen of Albert G. Gardner, in which the principal statement was related to him by his father, Joshua Gardner: "Many of the early settlers were of Puritan stock, and thoroughly imbued with the love of liberty, united to dauntless courage and daring to aid or rescue from oppression any helpless fellow being. But to the story.

One morning in the early part of summer of the year 1825 a party of neighbors were at the blacksmith shop of Joseph Giles, near New Lima, among whom was Joshua Gardner, the father of Albert, who lived near. A horseman was seen approaching from the direction of Scipio, and as he came fully in view it was seen that a negro woman sat on the horse with the stranger. It was evident that she was not a willing passenger on that train, so they were promptly halted. Mr. Gardner demanded of the man his authority for taking the woman. He had none. He said that "she acknowledged herself to be a slave of the Wagners in Virginia," opposite Kerr's run in Ohio. She had made her escape from bondage and was on her way to Canada to join her husband, who had made the race for freedom some time before. Thereupon Mr. Gardner told them that he was a peace officer, a town constable, and it was his duty to prevent kidnapping as well as other crimes. Turning to the woman, he asked her "if she wanted to go with this man." She almost sobbed out, "No, sir." Mr. Gardner told her to "get down and go where you please," and as an officer of the law he would protect her. She slipped down from the horse and started to retrace the road she came. The man started for Virginia to inform the Wagners and to put them on her track. Some of the party from the shop soon overtook the woman and guided her to the house of one Crandle, a poor man, but noble citizen, who lived in an "out of the way" place, where she could be provided for until the search and excitement should die away. The colored woman was hidden in an old brush fence by a shelving rock and fed and well taken care of by Mrs. Crandle and family. The Wagners were soon in the neighborhood, scouring the country and offering rewards. On one occasion a very poor man from the east side of the township came loitering around the premises of Crandle in search of deer or turkey and discovered the hiding place of the woman. Tempted by the reward offered, he started to inform the slave owners, but, as little souls are apt to be ignorant, stopped at Stephen Ralps' and told him of his plan and visions of future wealth. As soon as he left, Ralph shouldered his rifle and, marching through the woods, gave the alarm. Next morning the fire had destroyed the old brush fence and effaced all traces of its recent occupant. The Wagners concluded the old hunter was a wilful fraud. However, the woman was removed to the farm of Benjamin Bellows and secreted until he had communicated with parties in Canada and ascertained the whereabouts of the woman's husband. Mr. Bellows prepared a wagon with a false bottom, or double box, into the bottom of which he put the woman and on the top a lot of weavers' reeds and started for Canada to sell reeds. Mr. Bellows reported that he traveled one day with one of the Wagners and another party who were hunting this very woman, and that Mr. Wagner got off from his horse and helped Bellows' wagon down a steep, rocky hill to keep it from turning over, little suspecting that the object of his search was so near him.

Foiled in all other points, the Wagners determined to try the law to obtain the value of their woman chattel from Joshua Gardner. Suit was brought in Court of Common Pleas at Chester and came to trial by jury, which resulted in a verdict for the plaintiffs. An appeal was taken, and the Supreme Court held that the admissions and sayings of the woman could not be admitted to prove her identity; if she was a competent witness she must be produced in court; but if she was a slave she could not be a competent witness. So the case failed.

After the trial, Judge Pease, of the Supreme Court, was heard to say "that an action of trover for the recovery of stock might do in Virginia, but it would not do in Ohio unless the stock had more than two legs." M. Bosworth.

The next step was to kidnap Gardner and deal with him according to the rules of chivalry. It was reported that twelve men were seen on horseback in disguise for that purpose, but they were anticipated by a force abundantly able to resist them. There was no attack made. The expenses of this suit and trouble consequent consumed all of Mr. Gardner's property. He made an overland trip to California and obtained money sufficient to buy a comfortable home in Rutland, Ohio, where he enjoyed the respect and confidence of his neighbors.

Mr. Joshua Gardner was born in Connecticut January 5th, 1793, and died in Rutland March 1st, 1869, aged seventy-six years. Mrs. Gardner was Nancy, the daughter of James E. Caldwell, who came with his family from Vermont in 1817.

Albert Gallatin Gardner was born in Rutland March 15th, 1820. He contributed the foregoing narrative of Joshua Gardner. He married Lucy Bellows November 27th, 1849, and had a family of six children.

Albert G. Gardner died in Rutland, Ohio, January 13th, 1891, aged seventy years, ten months and twenty-eight days.

From the "Leader," by Mr. Charles Matthews, Washington, D. C., February, 1908:

"Daniel and Timothy Smith, with their brother-in-law, Bradbury Robinson, came from Vermont in 1805. With their families, household goods, wagons and stock, they floated down the Ohio river, stopping at Belpre, Big Hocking and Leading creek. The party, after looking at land and visiting the settlements, concluded to separate. Timothy Smith and family were landed at Silver run, while Daniel Smith and their brother-in-law, having purchased their brother's share in the boat, floated down the river to Cincinnati. Timothy Smith was born in 1770, and married Polly Conner, who was born in 1772. They had seven children, as follows: Charlotta Smith, born May 24th, 1797, and married Elias Jones in October, 1814; she died October 4th, 1871. John Adams Smith, born February 22nd, 1800, and married Deborah Paine, November 22nd, 1822; he died January 10th, 1840. Elizabeth Smith, born January 9th, 1802, and married John S. Giles June 7th, 1818; she died November 8th, 1842. Sarah Smith, born July 10th, 1804, and married Obadiah Ralph, September 19th, 1822; she died February 3rd, 1875. Anselin Smith, born in 1806, and died in 1816. Timothy Smith, Jr., born 1810, and died at the age of nine months. Mary Smith, born December 19th, 1812, and married Moses R. Matthews, April 10th, 1831; she died December 24th, 1893.

Timothy Smith erected one of the first grist mills in the county. It was a tread mill, run by horse power, located on the bank of Silver Run. He also mined the first coal, shipping to Cincinnati on a raft. John Adams Smith, above mentioned, was the man arrested by Virginia officials and confined in Point Pleasant jail for running off slaves, and was rescued by his Ohio friends in 1824, described in the paper by John S. Giles, Jr., so ably for the Pioneer Society and published in the "Telegraph" in 1875.

"In 1823 Hamilton Kerr, living at the mouth of Leading creek, employed Adams Smith to act as guide for eight colored men who were on their way to Canada, a not infrequent occurrence for colored persons made free by their masters to pass through the country on their way to Canada. So Mr. Smith escorted the colored men to Columbus as hired by Mr. Kerr, with no thought of wrong doing. The fact was that Kerr had given aid to colored people, bond or free, to go north. Slave owners on the Kanawha and on the Ohio river above Point Pleasant had organized for protection and sent out detectives on both sides of the river. They concluded that Smith was guilty of aiding escaped slaves. In October, 1824, four men from Virginia arrested Smith without authority of a warrant or law and took him by force into Virginia, and placed him in close confinement in the jail at Point Pleasant, refusing bail for him. This gross violation of the most sacred rights of the citizens of Ohio, showing such contempt for the state's jurisdiction that it excited universal indignation, and open violence was threatened to release Smith from his illegal confinement. Many good citizens of Ohio, who had no disposition to interfere with their Virginia neighbors in holding slaves, had no doubt often unconsciously aided slaves many times in giving them food or answering questions as to the points of compass when the traveling black man appeared at their doors, so it was argued that if one man, like Smith, upon whom suspicion had fallen, could be picked up without form of law and carried beyond the jurisdiction of the state and there imprisoned without the right of bail for a supposed criminal offense, what security was there for others equally exposed? This argument had its effect upon the excited people, and to the formation of a vigilance committee, with regular station signals from Colonel Jones' landing, where the Grant's mill stood, in Middleport, and from Smith's landing at the mouth of Silver run out to where John S. Giles lived in Rutland. So perfect was the arrangement that by the sound of horns transmitted from station to station, an alarm would circulate over the route in fifteen minutes if any suspicious person or company were seen at any of these points. Smith had been detained at Point Pleasant jail six weeks, during which time a plan had been matured to effect his release by force. John S. Giles had visited him in jail, ostensibly to take him clothing, but in fact to notify him of the arrangement and to be ready at any moment. Information that was considered reliable came from Point Pleasant of a plot to murder Smith in jail. It was said that one of the Wagners had put one of his slaves in the jail with Smith, who, in consideration of his freedom, was to commit the murder. On receipt of this information hasty preparations were made to carry into effect the plan for Smith's release.

"It was secretly arranged that Martin Meeker, William Hatch, John Woods, David Tyler, Obediah Ralph, William Terry, Charles Giles and John S. Giles to meet on the bank of the river at the mouth of Silver run on the evening of a day in November, 1824. These men were noted among the early settlers for their coolness, courage and great physical strength and activity. They had taken the greatest precaution in withdrawing from their homes without the knowledge of other members of their families. All were armed to the teeth with hunting rifles, pistols. One carried a flint lock musket loaded with seven rifle bullets, another carried a dragoon or horse-pistol loaded with three rifle bullets. They agreed on their plan and chose John S. Giles as commander, and, having disguised themselves by blacking their faces, they embarked in an old pirogue and with muffled oars floated down the river on their perilous adventure. It was known that the jail at Point Pleasant was strongly guarded, but these men, smarting under the outrage of their rights as citizens of Ohio, and aroused to resentment by the frequent taunts of Yankee cowardice hurled at them because they did not come and 'take Smith out,' as they had threatened to do, with fears for the imminent danger of the prinoner's life, had become desperate in their purposes. The little craft was urged forward by the long, dull strokes of the oars and landed eleven miles below at Point Pleasant. The jail was a two-story frame building, standing about fifty yards from the river bank, with two rooms below and two rooms above. The front entrance opened into the jailer's room on the lower floor, from which there was a passage into the other lower room, occupied as the jail. An outside stairs led to the rooms on the second floor, at the top of which was a platform, surrounded by bannisters and was used as a guard stand. The room at the head of the stairs was called the 'debtor's room.' On this occasion it was occupied by the guards, whose number had been increased to four men after the visit of Mr. John S. Giles. Without a word the attacking party divided, to make a simultaneous assault on the jailer's room and upon the upper room occupied by the guards. Meeker and Lyles reached the guards' room, where they succeeded so as to find an entrance for the muzzles of their guns, but the four guards inside held the door, but the action in placing the guns was menacing enough to restrain for a few minutes the guardmen, while the work in the lower room was in progress. First into the jailor's room, who was in bed, and just wakened, he was kept quiet by the presence of guns pointing close to him, while with an ax the prison door was broken down, and Smith jerked out of bed half asleep, and pushed through the door. The object of the raid having been effected so far, and no one hurt, they made haste to retreat and reach the boat as soon as possible. But the guards were out on the platform. Woods, with his dragoon's pistol, fired; the gun failed, but his audacity kept the guard back, thus enabling the party to gain time in advance of their pursuers, for the jailer, as well as the guard, were bold, brave men, and followed with such determined steps that the order was given to fire on the pursuing force. Terry fired with his musket and hit one of the guard, who fell, the ball having marked his ear and cut through his whiskers. Thus hindered, but while the Giles men were getting into their boat, the guardsmen stood on the top of the bank not more than forty yards away and began to fire. Disregarding the firing they pulled for the opposite shore until near the middle of the river when balls began to strike the boat with precision. The boat was turned broadside to the shore and the men lay close down in the side of the vessel until out of range of the firing, all but Tyler, who refused to obey this command to shelter himself, and received a ball across the lower part of his breast that made a scar four or five inches long. While holding the boat in this position and floating down stream, out of the range of guns, the jailer had taken a position behind a sycamore on the edge of the bank, and his shots were very annoying. His head looked like a knot on the side of the tree. And Hatch, the marksman of the company, was ordered to fire at the knot. He shot, and the ball, striking the side of the tree, filled the jailer's eyes with splinters. When reaching the Ohio shore, the boat was abandoned, and the men walked home, and before daylight crept to their beds so quietly that the members of their several households were not aware of their having been away or absent. The Virginians suspicioned John Woods, John S. Giles and Elisha Ayers, as three of the party that had broken the jail in Point Pleasant, and threats were heard of taking these men to Virginia, as they did Smith, and lynching them. This was not done. A more peaceful and lawful way was adopted, by seeking redress for their wrongs in the power of the law. Indictments were found at Point Pleasant against Woods, Ayers and Giles, and the Governor of Virginia made requisition on the Governor of Ohio for the surrender of the parties to the Virginia authorities. The Governor of Ohio issued his warrant and deputized Col. Lewis, of Virginia, to serve it. When Col. Lewis crossed the river to make the arrests, the people unaware of his authority, prepared to make a defense. Col. Lewis went directly to Chester, the county seat of Meigs county, and called to his assistance Thomas Rairdon, of Long Bottom, Deputy Sheriff Newsom and Constable Dickey, of Chester township. They went to make the first arrest of John S. Giles in Rutland and satisfied him of their authority, and he went without resistance, but they had not proceeded half a mile, when twelve men in disguise stepped out of the woods on Sargent's hill and demanded Giles' release. After some parleying, Giles convinced them of the authority from the Governor of the State that this was a legal transaction, and he was willing to let the law take its course, and they concluded to acquiesce. Among the men who were about to interfere were John Sylvester, Sr., Joshua Gardner, David Tyler and

Burrell Peck. Giles, Woods and Ayres were taken to Point Pleasant and lodged in jail, where they remained two months before they were tried.

Giles and Ayres were found "not guilty," but Woods was pronounced guilty and fined thirty dollars, which he refused to pay, or allow his friends to pay, and boarded it out in jail, refusing to leave until they would keep him no longer. Judge Summers, of Charleston, presided at the trial, which was a perfectly fair one. Judge Clough, of Portsmouth, and Judge Fisher, of Point Pleasant, were attorneys for the defendants.

There was no evidence whatever against Ayres, and none against Giles except the testimony of the jailer's wife, who swore positively to his being one of the party that broke into the room, but the jury was led to distrust her statement by the strong evidence of an alibi proven by the defendant. Polly Smith, a sister to Adams Smith, and afterwards the wife of Moses Matthews, a girl then of twelve years, and Col. Everett also gave strong evidence for the defendants which was all owing to the sly movements of the party in coming and going.

After the conviction of Woods, the defendants made a point that it was only a misdemeanor punishable by a fine and imprisonment in the county jail, and the court concurred in that opinion. A number of persons were presented to the grand jury of Meigs county for interfering with Col. Lewis when making arrests. Some were indicted but the evidence was not strong enough to warrant a conviction.

John S. Giles, Sr., was born in Maine, February 28th, 1795, and died in Rutland, O., May 18th, 1889, aged 86 years, 2 months and 20 days."

William Church was a native of Maine, was married twice. His first wife died, leaving two children—Samuel and Rhoda. Mr. Church married for his second wife a sister of the first wife, and a family of six sons and two daughters were born to them. He moved from Maine in 1816, with a family of seven sons and one daughter, and came to Rutland, O., in 1817. He was a millwright, and lived in Rutland until his death in 1821. The children were: Samuel, a millwright, a fine mechanic, who lived and died in Pomeroy, O. Clement Church was a mechanic and a farmer. He lived and died in Rutland, leaving several children. William Church lived and died in Rutland. Joseph Church had a paralytic stroke when quite a young man, but lived to marry and rear a large family of children. He settled in Salisbury township. John Church went to Minnesota, owned a farm and brought up a family. He died in Minnesota. Oliver Church moved to Marion county, O., and had a good farm, and died there at the age of ninety years, leaving a number of descendants. Alfred Church moved to Illinois, where he owned a mill and carried on that business until his death. Charles Church lived in Pomeroy, and was killed by the explosion of a boiler in the Pomeroy rolling mill in 1866.

Sarah Church was married to Curtis Larkin, who died in 1898, leaving a widow and one son, George B. Larkin, with whom she has a home, and lives in the enjoyment of good health, in her ninety-first year. 1908. G. B. L.

Clement Church married Hannah Buxton, who was born in England November 2, 1808, and came to Ohio in 1817, and became the wife of Clement Church in November, 1829. They had six children, three sons and three daughters—Royal Church and James Church, and Mrs. Maria Shepherd and Mrs. Eliza Thompson. Mrs. Hannah Church died in August, 1896, aged 87 years, 9 months, 6 days.

Mrs. Elizabeth Church, widow of William Church, Sr., was married to John Hoyt, and died in July, 1859; was buried at Hoyt Town, Meigs county, Ohio.

There are many families of the name of Hoyt in Olive township and Orange, but no record of names or dates have been furnished for Mr. Larkin's manuscript, and the same fact is evident in the lack of family history of the name of Stout in and about Chester township. Their names are always associated with the reputation of citizens of the best influence and character.

RANDALL STIVERS.

Randall Stivers was born in New Jersey and was the son of Daniel Stivers, a Revolutionary soldier. Mr. Stivers married Phebe Ball, a native of Vermont, and a daughter of Samuel Ball, a Revolutionary soldier. They came with four children to Graham's Station (now Racine), in 1816, having come from Olean, N. Y., on a raft of pine lumber.

He was a brickmaker by trade, and found employment in that business at Graham Station, remained there for two years. Hearing of the discovery of coal, easily accessible, and near the Ohio river bank at Kerr's run, he removed to that place, where they lived three years. In those first five years in Ohio they experienced the privations and hardships as fully as generally fall to the lot of early emigrants. In a sparsely settled neighborhood, with barely sufficient means for support as the common lot of the people, they built a school-house and hired teachers. In 1819, the new county of Meigs was organized, and about 1821 the county seat was located at Chester, to which place Mr. Stivers removed his family in 1822. He was elected Justice of the Peace in Chester, and held the office for several years. He served four years as Sheriff, and was twice elected to the State Legislature. He was a promotor and patron of schools, and always interested in churches and works of benevolence. He was fearless in expressing his sentiments, and society and public affairs felt the influence of his opinions. Mr. Randall Stivers and his wife reared a large family, all of whom were prominent in business, or in political and educational lines. There were six sons and four daughters.

Washington Stivers was married twice. Julia Stanley was his first wife, and Caroline Fisher the second. He was a merchant, and sold goods in Pomeroy for a number of years.

Afterwards he moved to Chattanooga, Tenn., where he died in ripe old age.

Aaron Stivers was married twice; the first wife was Miss Kerr; the second, Miss Cole. Mr. Aaron Stivers was one of the best known men in Meigs county, serving as Auditor and Deputy Auditor for many years. He made and published a large wall map of the county, suitable for school-houses, a work of thoroughly correct presentation.

He was one of the most active members of the Meigs County Pioneer Association, and served as its Recording Secretary for seven years. He removed to Alton, Iowa, where he died November 29th, 1893, aged 77 years.

Katharine Stivers was married to Theodore Montague, a lawyer who lived in Chester until the county seat was taken to Pomeroy, when they removed to Middleport, and continued as useful members of society for many years. In later life they made their home in Chattanooga, and there they both died.

Serena Stivers became the wife of Mr. Allen, of Middleport, and died in middle life, leaving a husband and interesting family.

George Stivers married in Meigs county, but moved west. He was a soldier in the Civil war, and died soon afterward.

William Stivers went from Chester to Indiana, married there, and had a family. He was engaged in business, and was elected to the legislature, serving with credit to himself and constituents. He died in Indiana.

Charles Stivers settled in Kentucky, where he married.

Randall Stivers was the youngest son, and accompanied his father, Randall Stivers, Sr., to California on the overland route in 1849, and died in California.

Urania Stivers was born in Chester, December 25th, 1827, and received her education in the Academy at Chester, and later in a prosperous seminary in Ashland, Kentucky. In her early teens she became a teacher in the public schools in

Meigs county. She taught many years in the Pomeroy schools, a highly respected and successful teacher.

Caroline Stivers, the younger sister, acquired her education in the same schools with her sister Urania, and was also a popular school teacher, yet she was employed in the office of the Auditor, with her brother Aaron Stivers for several consecutive years. These sisters left Meigs county in 1884, and finally located in Des Moines, Iowa. Their influence for right principles and useful lives was evident through all the years as teachers in Pomeroy, Ohio, as well as in less active years in Des Moines, Iowa.

Randall Stivers, Sr., and his wife, Phebe B. Stivers, both died in Pomeroy, and are buried side by side in the beautiful Beech Grove Cemetery.

Pioneer travel on the Ohio river, for neighborly intercourse, or traffic, seems to have been done in canoes, while flatboats were in use for the transportation of families, produce and goods down the stream; but when it was necessary to carry on trade up and down the river, keel-boats were employed, until steamboat navigation superseded their mode as merchant carriers. The first steamboat that ever passed down the Ohio river is said to have been the New Orleans, built at Pittsburg by Mr. Roosevelt, and which left that port in October, 1811, and reached Natchez, Miss., in January, 1812. Earthquakes occurred during the trip down. Few charts of the river were in existence, and the falls at Letart were provided with a pilot appointed by Congress, or rather authorizing the courts of Gallia county to appoint a pilot for Letart falls to pilot boats over the falls in the Ohio river, such pilot to give bonds for the proper discharge of his duty. Thomas Sayre was appointed in 1804 as such pilot.

Adam Harpold was born October 9, 1790, and came to Letart, O., in 1812, where he married Dorothy Roush in August, 1812. They settled on a farm, and Mr. Harpold conducted a store, the first one for dry goods and groceries in Letart township. After the county of Meigs was organized and Courts of Common Pleas were held in the meeting-house in Salisbury township—in the July term of 1819, among the jurors impaneled is the name of Adam Harpold. He was prominent in township offices and a patron of education, strictly honest in business transactions, and maintained the respect and confidence of the community. Mrs. Harpold was a woman of strong character, of wonderful physical power and vitality. They had a family of sixteen children, and all save one child, who was drowned at seven years of age—seven sons and eight daughters—grew up and married, each making a new home of thrift and industry. The sons were mostly farmers and have been identified with the material prosperity of Meigs county for more than sixty years. Henry Harpold, Spencer Harpold, Peter Harpold, Philip Harpold, William Harpold, George B. Harpold, John Harpold. The daughters: Mrs. Pickens, widow, later Mrs. Wolf; Mrs. William Hester, widow, Mrs. Jacob Baker; Mrs. Michael Bentz, neé Polly Harpold; Mrs. Eben Sayre, Mrs. Augustus Justice, Mrs. Hezekiah Quillen, Mrs. Bradford Roush, Mrs. Barbara Ann McDade.

The greater number of the Harpold sons and daughters had large families, so that the descendants in the third and fourth generations were notably numerous.

Mr. Adam Harpold died in October, 1869, and his wife, Mrs. Dorothy Harpold, died in December, 1865, having lived in their Letart home for more than fifty years.

"At a meeting of the associate judges of the county of Gallia, held at Gallipolis the tenth day of May, 1803, for the purpose of dividing the county of Gallia into townships and to apportion to each township a proper number of justices of the peace, and for other purposes; present, Robert Safford and George W. Putnam.

"The said county was divided into three townships, named and bounded as follows: Letart township, beginning at the mouth of Shade river; thence down the Ohio river to Kerr's run; thence north to the county line; thence east with the said line to the place of beginning; and that one justice of the peace is the proper number to be elected in said township, and that the election be held at the house of Henry Roush." From Gallia county records.

From the foregoing we find that Henry Roush, Sr., lived in Letart township in 1803, but at what date he came to Ohio we are not informed.

Henry Roush, Sr., owned land in Letart, Ohio, opposite Letart Falls, and brought up a large family.

His son, Henry Roush, Jr., entered land in 1808, or purchased of the Ohio Land Company's Purchase, thirty-seven acres, as shown by the Gallia county records. He married Anna Sayre, of Mill Creek, Va., and settled on their farm in Letart, where they had a family of ten daughters and two sons. Sally Roush was married to Thomas Coleman, of Muses Bottom, W. Va. Betsy was the wife of Samuel Roberts, later married Henry Wolf, of Racine. Lydia was married twice—to Charles McClain—widow—Mr. Wagner. Anna was the wife of Mark Sayre; lived and died in Great Bend, Ohio. Hannah was married to Mr. Coleman; a widow—married—Mr. Jackson. Dorothy was the wife of Silas Jones, a prominent member of the Pioneer Association. Phebe was married to Elijah Runner, a son of an early settler of that name. Katharine was the wife of Morris Greenlee. Almena was married to Jacob Brinker, of West Virginia. Mahala was the wife of a Mr. Quillen.

Edward Roush married Julia Sparr; moved to Illinois and died. David Roush married Maria Hayman; moved to Grand Rapids; is dead.

Mr. Henry Roush, Jr., died at an advanced age, and his wife, Mrs. Anna Roush, attained the remarkable age of 105 years at her decease. They were worthy people, and their children were all esteemed members of society.

Mrs. Dorothy Harpold was a daughter of Henry Roush, Sr.

Paper by Mr. Charles Matthews, of Washington, D. C., as published in the Leader, March 12th, 1908:

"Among the earliest settlers of Meigs county was George Washington Putnam, son of Colonel Israel Putnam and grandson of General Israel Putnam. George W. Putnam was born in Pomfret, Conn., July 27th, 1777. After the Indian war he came to Ohio with his father and his family, driving one of the teams, along with the late Phineas Matthews, of Cheshire, who also drove one of Colonel Putnam's teams. George W. Putnam was married March 31st, 1799, to Lucinda Oliver, daughter of Colonel Alexander Oliver, of Washington county, and settled on lands then in Washington county, now located mostly in Gallia county, but the fraction of land on which he built his house is now located in Meigs county, on what is known as the Jacob Coughenour farm, between the turnpike and the river and from the Carl coal railway down the river to where the township line strikes the river. He also owned two 100-acre lots, Nos. 392 and 395, immediately west, now in Cheshire township. His dwelling stood on the lower part of the fraction of land now in Meigs county, where he lived and died before Meigs county was formed.

Their children were Sarah, Lucretia, George W., Jr., Isabel and Clarinda. Sarah married Henry Sisson, February 16th, 1818. He was killed by the falling of a tree January 10th, 1827. George W. Putnam was the first county judge of Gallia county. He died in May, 1815, of what was known as the "cold plague." Whatever that may have been, it was certainly contagious, for the reason that Mrs. Mary (Russell) Matthews, first wife of Phineas Matthews, who volunteered to help attend their old friend during his illness and until his death, was then herself taken with the same disease and died in a short time. Another version of his death is that he was

CHARLES MATTHEWS

helping Phineas Matthews shear his sheep, became overheated, drank too much cold water and was taken with the "cold plague" and died at the Matthews farm house. Mrs. Matthews nursed him, took the same disease and died within a week (June 4th, 1815), leaving an infant son, a few days less than two months old.

Mr. Putnam was buried on his farm, and several of his family were afterwards buried beside him. His unmarked grave is located immediately below the Carl coal railway, about half way from the turnpike to the river. Formerly there was a tombstone at his grave, but about four years ago some of his relatives bought a lot in the Gravel Hill Cemetery, Cheshire township, and moved the tombstone to that cemetery, but did not remove the remains of Mr. Putnam or his family. The grave can yet be located by Mr. Coughenour or W. P. Cohen or his mother. The son has repeatedly told me that he "would be willing to undertake to remove his remains to Gravel Hill Cemetery." Copied by E. L. B.

Tumuli or mounds were seen in various localities, always bearing evidence of man's work in their construction; always conical in shape and usually situated on the top of hills, as favorable to watch tower use. The curiosity of many settlers, ignorant and otherwise, despoiled these peculiar mounds by digging them down to find what might be entombed within. Human skeletons, pottery, mica and stone axes, copper rings, were exhumed in most places. There were in Lebanon township several mounds, one on the Bicknell farm that had a well defined fortification in the shape of a horseshoe surrounding the mound at a regular distance from the base. This mound was never opened, but, being in a field of level land, was plowed over, and very much of the hill shape was leveled. A larger mound on the James Hall farm was opened, and human bones, trinkets of copper, mica and curious stone arrows, pipes and stone axes were disclosed. In Rutland township was a large mound on the hill near the center of Section No. 7. It was twelve feet high, and the bones of a very large man were found there. A small one on white clay bottom was on the Stevens farm; also one on the southeast quarter of Section No. 8. A large mound on fraction No. 13 was known as the one on which Samuel Denny stood and made an oration July 4th, 1806.

According to the measurements and calculations by a civil engineer, Henry Grayum, in 1873, the principal coal seam in Meigs and Gallia county has a dip to the east of about twenty-seven feet and to the south five feet to the mile. The greatest elevation in the measurements taken was at Braley's salt well, 840 feet, and its least at Antiquity, 377 feet, a difference of 463 feet in the direction of tidewater at Norfolk, Va.

Samuel Denny was a prominent actor in nearly all the public transactions on Leading creek, and by many persons his name was supposed to be Dana, but the reading of his letters and business accounts show that he subscribed his name as Samuel Denny.

Livingston Smith was the son of Noah Smith and his wife and was born in Vermont in 1796, but came with his mother to Leading creek, Ohio, in 1800, his father, Noah Smith, having died in Carlisle, Pa., while moving with his family to Ohio. Livingston grew up to manhood, married Eliza Case and settled on a farm in Rutland township and reared a family. Mr. Smith was a good citizen, intelligent and esteemed by the community, and lived and died in Rutland township. Virgil C. Smith was the son of Livingston Smith and was born November 28th, 1833, and married Mary Plummer in 1857, who died in 1875. He was married the second time, to Agnes C. Torrence, in 1876. He was a farmer and also a minister of the Christian Church. He lived in Rutland and was identified with every enterprise for the moral elevation of the dependent and neglected. He was the recording secretary of the Pioneer Society of Meigs county at the time of his death, in March, 1885, a man loved by his friends and respected by his neighbors. He left a widow and seven children.

Mrs. Noah Smith, the mother of Iivingston Smith, came from Vermont to Leading Creek, Ohio, with three daughters, besides the son, heretofore mentioned. They were: Theresa, who was married to Eliezer Barker, who was drowned in Leading creek in June, 1813. She afterwards was Mrs. Laundress Grant. Jenny Smith married a Mr. Maples. Nancy Smith became the wife of Captain Jesse Hubbell.

William Johnson was born in Ireland and married Sally Harmon. They emigrated to the United States and came to Shade river in Chester township in 1800. There they made a home, in which they raised a large family. This was a religious family, and all lived to honor their pious parentage. Abram Johnson was a local preacher, and Thomas Johnson moved west. Mary was the wife of John Miles. Adaline, Mrs. Henry Ellis. Sarah, Mrs. John Wolf. William Johnson and his wife died in 1836 and 1848.

John Entsminger was born in Virginia in September, 1757, and when but a youth of seventeen years was an active participant in the battle at Point Pleasant under the immediate command of Colonel Charles Lewis. He was a soldier in the Revolutionary War under General Francis Marion and subsequently under General Morgan. He fought at the battle of Cowpens. Many incidents of soldier life were related by him in later years to his children. Mr. Enstminger was captured by the British at one time, but released on condition that he would go home and fight no more. A comrade, whose name was Vansant, and he started home, but on the way they came across several Tories who were building a house and who twitted them about having been captured. They went on a little farther, when Mr. Entsminger said to his comrade, "I wish we had thrashed them," and, going on a little farther, he said, "Let's go back and thrash them." So they turned back and whipped the Tory men, took them prisoners and marched with them to the Continental army and again took up arms and served until the close of the war for independence. John Entsminger married Jane Reese, February 16th, 1787. She was born on July 26th, 1759. They moved with their family from Botetourt county, Va., to Ohio, in the fall of 1797. They traveled overland, bringing their stock and household goods with them. They would travel all day and camp at night. Sometimes stopping a day to cook and bake, when necessary. They milked their cows, and after using what milk they wanted put the rest of it in the churn, set the churn in the wagon, and the butter was ready to take out when they stopped at night. They crossed the Ohio river about five miles above where Gallipolis now stands, known then as French Town. At that time, leaving out the primitive town, there was but one house besides theirs in a radius of ten miles on the Ohio side of the river. They ground corn on hand mills and went to Logan for flour. Later they could buy flour from the canoemen who poled their crafts up stream. Salted bear meat and fresh game supplied their tables. Although fifty-five years of age, Mr. Entsminger volunteered and served a term under General Tupper in 1812 in the Northwest. His eldest son, David Entsminger, was a soldier in the War of 1812. Mr. John Entsminger and his wife had a family of two sons and four daughters. David, John Lewis. The daughters were: Mrs. Luther Shepherd, Mrs. John Bing, Mrs. Daniel Grayum and Mrs. David Grayum, who was left a widow with two daughters and two sons. Henry Grayum served as major in the Civil War; William Grayum was a captain in the Fourth West Virginia from the first to the close of the war in 1865. Mr. John Entsminger felt crowded when the settlers moved into that neighborhood, so he went farther into the wilderness

Stone House Built by Luther Donaldson, a Revolutionary Soldier, the Home of his old age.

and located near where Langsville is now and lived there with his son, John Lewis Entsminger, until the close of his eventful life, on October 10th, 1830, fifty-six years to a day from the celebrated battle of Point Pleasant, aged seventy-eight years. He was buried in the Miles Cemetery. Mrs. Jane Entsminger died May 19th, 1830, in the seventy-first year of her age, and is buried in the Miles Cemetery at Rutland, Ohio.

George Wolfe, father of John, Jacob, Peter and Henry Wolfe, came from the Shenandoah valley of Virginia to the rich bottom lands on the Ohio river adjoining the present village of Racine, about 1807 or 1808, date uncertain. He felled the great trees and toiled hard to clear land for cultivation, and in 1812 his sons, John Wolfe and Jacob Wolfe, who had families, emigrated to Ohio. John Wolfe, with a four-horse covered wagon, came over the Alleghany mountains to inherit the home founded by the father, George Wolfe. There were two younger brothers, Peter and Henry Wolfe. John Wolfe and Jacob Wolfe built each of them a two-story brick house on the river front of their respective farms and reared large families. They tilled the land, planted fruit trees and lived to see a numerous posterity grow up around their homes, a quiet, honest, industrious people. The Wolfe bottoms have been owned and cultivated by the descendants of George Wolfe for at least one hundred years. In recent years the families have been distributed over other sections of the country.

The first Regular Baptist Church in Rutland was organized on November 27th, 1817, by members signing the covenant, seven men and three women. Benjamin Richardson, clerk, and Thomas Everton, deacon. The church was further organized on October 31st, 1818, by the following persons signing the covenant: Thomas Everton, Asahel Skinner, Anson Gaston, Benjamin Richardson, Robert Simpson, Relief Everton,

Betsy Richardson, Elizabeth Holt, Thomas Gaston, Jared Gaston, Ebenezer Everton, Laundress Grant, William Stevens, Joseph Richardson, Sally Stevens, Bethiah Simpson.

The first preachers were Aaron Holt, Peter Aleshire, Horace Persons and Thomas Gaston. Afterwards other ministers preached at different times—James Hovey, Amos Stevens and James McAboy. The brick schoolhouse was used for religious worship by several denominations—the Free Will Baptists, Presbyterians, Methodists, Regular Baptists and Universalists. The Presbyterians built a church on the lot by the Plummer homestead in 1820, it being the first church erected in Rutland township. The Regular Baptists built their church in 1838. Benjamin Richardson gave the lot and did a large share toward building the house. The first Disciples, or Christian church, in Rutland was built on a lot given by Rev. Elisha Rathburn.

Rutland Cemetery was surveyed and laid out in lots in 1824 by Samuel Halliday. The place had been used as a burying ground for a long time, but the interments had been made without regularity, so that it was difficult to make the proper arrangement of the premises when surveyed by Mr. Halliday. The lots were made 8 by 33 feet in size. Later, in 1872, the township of Rutland bought of George McQuigg the cemetery grounds, which, including the "old graveyard," contains three and three-quarters acres of land. The size of the new lots, 10 by 24 feet, which are staked and numbered.

The first burial in what is now Rutland township, from the settlement in 1805, was that of a girl nine years of age and who was buried on the Higley farm, a spot afterwards abandoned, but a family burying place was made on the Higley grounds in subsequent years. Many persons were buried on the Phelps farm. Some of the pioneers were interred on their own land. The first grave made in the Miles' Cemetery was for a little child, but no date is known. Dr. Clark, from New England, came to Ohio in quest of health, and died soon after his arrival and was the second person buried there, but his grave was unmarked and the precise location is lost, as is many another one.

John Hayman and family came from Somerset county, Md., about 1810. They came first to Letart Falls, in Virginia, but soon removed to Letart, Ohio. Their eldest son was Spencer Marshall Hayman, who married Jerusha Chapman, a daughter of Ezra Chapman, an old settler in Letart township. Spencer M. Hayman was a surveyor and after the organization of Meigs county, was elected as surveyor for the county, and served the public in that office for many consecutive terms. He was also justice of the peace and the first postmaster at Apple Grove, so named because of Mr. Hayman's large orchard of fine fruit. They brought up a large family—three sons and five daughters. The sons were: Ezra Hayman, who married Sally Wright, of Mill Creek, W. Va., who lived and died in Letart township. Henry Hayman was married twice. His first wife was Minerva Marvin, a daughter of Calvin Marvin; the second wife was a Miss Harding. Henry Hayman lived in Mercer's Bottom, where he died. Harrison Hayman married Agnes Williamson, a daughter of Wilkinson D. Williamson, of Lebanon township, Meigs county, Ohio. They settled in Warth's Bottom, W. Va. Both are dead. The daughters: Sinai Hayman was the wife of Hillman Parr. Betsy Hayman was married to William McKay, of Warth's Bottom. Minerva was Mrs. Ephraim I. Sayre, of Letart township.

Martha Ann Hayman was married to Elson Paden, and their home was just below Letart Falls, in Ohio. They were noted for true Christian lives and benevolence.

Angeline Hayman was the wife of a Mr. Paden; both died early.

Kitty Hayman married James Ashworth. Both died soon.

Josiah Hayman was the second son of John Hayman and was in the family that moved from Maryland. He married Nancy Ford, a daughter of Mrs. Esther Ford, a widow, who came from Maryland at the time of the senior Hayman's emigration to Ohio. Josiah Hayman lived in Letart township, where they brought up a large family. Mr. Hayman was a local preacher, belonging to the Methodist Episcopal Church, and a fine singer, noted for leading large congregations on camp grounds. They had a family of sons—Wesley, Henry, Calvin, Lewis, William and Charles; daughters—Elizabeth, Mary Ann, Regina and Adaline Esther. Wesley Hayman married Thirza Maria Cross, became insane, never recovered. Henry Hayman married Margaret Wagner and lived in Letart. He was a man highly esteemed by a large circle of friends and acquaintances. He was elected sheriff one or two terms. Always identified with the affairs of his church as steward, class leader and Sunday school superintendent. They reared a family of worthy citizens. Calvin and Lewis Hayman died in young manhood.

William Hayman, son of Josiah Hayman and his wife, was married to Mary Jane Donally, a daughter of Andrew B. Donally, many years clerk of the Court of Common Pleas, Meigs county. He made their home at Letart Falls, W. Va. Was a merchant. Esther Hayman became the wife of Lewis Pilchard; lived at Letart Falls. Elizabeth married John Ritchie, but died soon afterwards. Regina was the wife of Townsend Smart; lived in Racine and died there, leaving a family of five children—Arthur, Frank, William, Earl and one daughter.

Adaline Hayman was the wife of Philip Jones, of West Virginia.

Hezekiah Hayman was a nephew of John Hayman, Sr., and moved with his family from Maryland in company with his uncle to Ohio in about 1810. One son, Robert Hayman, lives in Middleport, Ohio. Stephen Hayman married Letitia Caldwell, and their children were: John N. Hayman, one of the commissioners of Meigs county for several terms; Stephen

Hayman, of Grand Island, Neb., and Maria, the widow of David Roush, who died at Grand Island, Neb.

John Wagner was born May 12th, 1792, and came to Letart, Ohio, from Lancaster, Pa., after the War of 1812. He was a soldier in that war. He married Elizabeth Himeleich in 1818 and settled in Letart, Ohio. They had three children—George H. Wagner, Alfred N. and Margaret, who became the wife of Henry Hayman, son of Josiah Hayman. Mrs. Elizabeth Wagner died in October, 1821. Mr. Wagner married a second wife, a widow, Mrs. Lydia McClain, and they had two children. Mr. John Wagner died in March, 1882, and Mrs. Lydia Wagner died at ninety years of age.

George Burns came from Philadelphia to Letart, Ohio, at an early day. Had charge of a floating mill at Letart Falls and kept a store, said to be the first at Letart, Ohio. There was a family of three daughters and one son, George Burns, Jr. The eldest daughter was Mrs. Alfred Beauchamp, of Elizabeth, W. Va. Caroline became the wife of Thomas Alexander, of Letart, and spent her long life in their home in Letart, where they brought up a family of eleven children. They were influential and highly respected people. They died at the advanced ages of eighty-four and ninety years. Regina Burns was married to John Caldwell and made a home in Letart, where they brought up a family. She died many years ago.

Obadiah Walker and Cassandra Walker, neé Halsey, lived in Chester township in 1805 and spent their long lives in the same locality. They were good citizens and brought up a large family of sons and daughters.

Jesse Walker, the eldest child, was born in 1806. He was twice married. Miss P. M. Richardson was the first wife, but dying, left two children. He then married Margaret Mauck, of Cheshire, Gallia county, where they made their home until death. They had two children. Jesse Walker died at the ripe age of eighty-five years, a kind, upright man, a member of the Free Will Baptist Church from his youth. Milton Walker married Harriet Newel and lived in Chester several years, and then went to Illinois. They were Methodists, earnest Christians. Selden Walker, Vincent Walker and Obadiah Walker were younger sons. Vincent married Sevilla Weldon and moved to Iowa and died there. Obadiah married Emily Weldon; lived and died in Chester township. Bethia Walker was the wife of Baza Wells, in Chester. She had two children, but buried them and her husband also. She was married afterwards to Benjamin Brown, of Athens, Ohio. All are dead.

Melissa Walker married and was left a widow in Iowa. Emeline Walker was the wife of William Church, in Rutland, Ohio, where he died, and she went to Iowa. Samaria Walker was married to James Decker, of Lebanon township. They had two or three children. Mr. Decker and Mrs. Decker died in Lebanon township. Caroline Walker was married to Abner Hissim, of Tanner's Run, Ohio, but later they removed to Iowa.

In the Gallia county records of deeds made for lands coming within the boundary of Meigs county when organized is the name of Thomas Halsey, purchaser, 1792. The family of Halsey have continued in Chester and Orange townships, with their descendants.

Dr. Fenn Robinson was the most noted doctor within the boundaries included in Meigs county in the pioneer days. He had an extensive practice, and he was equal to any emergency. His saddle pockets were receptacles for all medicines needed, with compartments for surgical instruments. He could pull a tooth or cut off a man's leg, if necessity required, lance an abscess or an arm, spread a fly blister plaster or set a dislocated joint. He rode through the woods, following road or trail, through creeks, at high or low tide, in rain or snow, at night or in the day—he found the way. His patients believed in him and had faith in his skill. His travels were in a radius of more than thirty miles from his home at Chester, and he was the family doctor for two or more generations. No trained nurse with sick folks then, nor pharmacist to fill prescriptions. He reared a large and highly respectable family. Dr. Robinson never ran for Congress nor sued a poor man for his bill. His honors rested on a noble life.

John Hall and his wife, Sarah Hall, nee Hahurst, came from Pennsylvania and settled on a tract of land in Letart township above the mouth of Old Town creek, known as Ohio river bottom land, in the year 1811. Mrs. Hall was reared by Quaker parents. They were industrious and thrifty and cleared for cultivation their large farm. They had a large family of sons and daughters.

James Hall, the eldest son, married Leah Ford, and they lived in Lebanon township and brought up a family. Their children were: William Henry Hall, Wesley, Thomas, Isaac Lewis, Spencer Marshall and a son Benjamin, who died in childhood. Two daughters were: Sarah, who was married to Hamilton Parr and lived in Brown county, Ohio. Ann Maria Hall died in young womanhood. James Hall was elected justice of the peace and served one or two terms. He was postmaster for Great Bend, Ohio, several years. He died in 1885 or 1886. Mrs. Hall lived to the great age of eighty-seven years, a most excellent woman. They both died in Great Bend, Ohio. Job Hall married Betsy Smith, daughter of Solomon Smith. She died early, leaving two children. Job Hall was killed on his boat on the Yazoo river, supposedly for money.

Ela Hall married Polly Lasley. John Hall married Silvina Buffington. Aaron Hall married Nancy Crall. The daughters were: Nancy Hall, the wife of Isaac Lauck, and moved to Missouri. Rachel was married to Ezra Lauck, and they went west. Matilda Hall was married twice—first to Mr. Shafer and afterwards to John Lee. She lived and died in Lebanon township. Mary Hall was Mrs. Owen Darby; they went west. Delilah was married to a Mr. Lornes and died in Great Bend. Sarah Ann was married three times. The first husband, George Cummings, who died. Mr. Ezekiel Custer, Sr., was the second husband, and John Warner third.

Mr. John Hall, Sr., died in middle age, but left a will that was the puzzle for lawyers for two generations. Mrs. Sarah Hall died in the early seventies, living and dying on their homestead farm.

The Sayres are a numerous people, residing in Letart, Ohio, and Letart, W. Va. David Sayre entered land in Letart township in 1803. There are several branches of the name, descendants in four and five generations, living in Meigs county. Daniel Sayre, father of Moses E. Sayre and great-grandfather to the Hon. Edgar Ervin, were first settlers in Letart township. As a people the Sayres were religious, good, prosperous citizens. Mr. Ervin is a member of the Ohio Legislature, a native of Meigs, and has reflected credit on his family and won popularity for his own public services in the Ohio Legislature for the years of 1907 and 1908.

At the pioneer meeting in August, 1890, Mr. Phineas Robinson made a speech, in which he said that "in early times silver was the coin most in use by the common people, and that it was often cut into four or five parts to make change," a fact that the writer of this article well remembers. Mr. Robinson also gave a history of the Keg Company of Chester, which was undoubtedly correct as he stated it, but not as published from report in the Telegraph. Therefore this reviewer wishes to state the case as he understands it.

About 1825 or 1826, not sure as to date, a company was formed, it was said, of Nathan Newsom, a tanner, who lived in Chester; Moses Green, of Orange township, said to be a horse jockey, who had married into a very respectable family; Nicholas Lake, who also had a very respectable woman for a wife, and John Nolan, a batchelor, who lived about Chester at that time, not a bad man naturally, but so constituted that he could be made a cat's paw when needed. The Keg Company made and sold counterfeit money, silver dollars, that could not be told from the genuine, and they would exchange two dollars for one good one. So one man, having two or three hundred dollars, agreed to buy of the spurious coin, and, repairing to a secret room, his money was counted out on a table, when the lights were suddenly put out and all the money swept off from the table. The man lost his money. He went before the grand jury, and the four men were indicted. They could not arrest Newsom and Green, they fleeing to parts unknown. An officer tried to arrest Nolan, who stabbed the officer and was sent to the penitentiary for it. As soon as he had served his time he left for New Orleans, where it was said that he became a wealthy and respectable citizen.

Lake had stolen a horse in Athens county and was sent to the penitentiary for that act. While in prison he, with others, was taken under guard outside to work. Lake attempted to run away, the guard shot and wounded him so that he died.

In 1818 Dr. David Gardner and his brother Charles came to Chester, Ohio. They bought out Mr. Levi Stedman's store and filled it with goods purchased in the Eastern cities. Charles Gardner went back to Long Island, New York, but Dr. Gardner remained in Chester many years and died there; also Mrs. Gardner, and both are buried in the Chester Cemetery. Their daughter was married to Mr. Maples, an Episcopal clergyman, who was rector of Grace Church in Pomeroy, Ohio, and influential in the erection of the neat Gothic church in that place.

After a long and successful pastorate, winning high regard for his character, he unfortunately became insane and died in the Athens Hospital for the Insane.

Edward Weldon was married to Mary Faris in Dublin, Ireland, and emigrated to the United States. The precise date is not on record, but they located for a few years in Washington county, Pa., where Mr. Edward Weldon died; also two sons, each one named Edward. The widow, Mrs. Weldon, moved first to the Lewis farm, above Point Pleasant, Va., and stayed one year, when she removed with her family to Chester, Ohio. The children were: Frank Weldon, who was lost, fate unknown. James Weldon married Lettie Stout. William Weldon married Elinor Pullins; lived and died in Chester, Ohio. John Weldon married Mary, daughter of Dr. Fuller Elliott; settled in Letart township, later Sutton, and had a family of sons and daughters. Richard Weldon, married Sally, daughter of Levi Stedman, of Chester. They had two daughters—Emily, Mrs. Obadiah Walker, and Caroline, who was married to Mr. Heaton. Richard Weldon and his wife died young. Martha Weldon became Mrs. Samuel McKinley; lived in Kentucky. Catharine was married to John Van Kirk, in Chester township. Margaret became the wife of Augustus Watkins.

Mary Weldon was the first wife of Andrew Donnelly, clerk of the Court of Common Pleas for Meigs county during a long period of years. Mrs. Donnelly died young, leaving two children, Charles Donnelly and Margaret.

Francis Weldon, son of James Weldon, married Rachel Cozad; parents of Mrs. Lurinda Williamson, widow of Captain James Williamson, now of California.

A remarkable meteoric shower was displayed in November of the year 1831. It was called "the stars falling," and created great alarm in some localities. Some people averred that the judgment day had come, while others opened their Bibles to read of "stars falling and men's hearts failing," while in many homes in sparsely settled places the inhabitants slept soundly and knew nothing of the wonderful sight in the heavens reported by witnesses.

Rev. Isaac Reynolds lived in Letart village and mingled with the frightened ones, allaying their fears. He said "the meteors fell thickly at one time, and that strange, fantastic shapes were assumed by many of those lurid bodies in their descent to the earth." The history of meteoric showers or the aerolites had not been taught in the schools. This event was generally concluded to foretell some great calamity to befall the world.

Another natural phenomena was considered as an omen of calamity—the aurora borealis, or northern light. The beauty of the sky was not so impressive as the smothered belief that some disaster was impending, as of war or pestilence.

A comet with a luminous following gave certain warning to a class of credulous folks that the end of this world was near, and a few believers in the Miller prophecy resided in Lebanon township. Time has gone on with great regularity; spring and summer, autumn and winter, have banished such fears.

A flood in the Ohio river in 1832 was a real and disastrous event. The inhabitants were living in houses on the river bank, and farmers especially had no buildings on the bluff or second bank to shelter themselves. In Lebanon several families sought shelter in a two-story log house, but the water continued rising, so that at nightfall they were removed in flatboats to the hillside, making beds on the ground in the open field, although snow was falling in scattering flakes. One man made a pen on his flatboat for his four fat hogs and for his chickens, with corn for feeding them. Stock and horses were taken to the hills before the water had wholly covered the bottom lands. Houses, barns, haystacks, as well as uprooted trees, went hurrying by on the swollen river.

Of the cholera in Chester in the year 1834 an account of the scourge was published in the Meigs County

Telegraph of January 20th, 1893, and copied from that paper into this manuscript the same year by S. C. Larkin. "Fifty-nine years ago since Meigs county had that awful experience with cholera. Chester was then the county seat and the chief village in the county, with a population of 200 souls. Of those who lived in Chester in 1834 but three persons remain as residents of the old village with clear remembrance of that event, Mrs. Dolly A. Knight, Mr. Harold Wells and E. Sardine Weldon, then a child of six years. Reports were in circulation of the ravages of Asiatic cholera in maritime cities, New York and New Orleans, and of its deadly prevalence in foreign countries. Mrs. Dolly Knight and her husband, Benjamin Knight, moved from the Ohio river, where Pomeroy was located later, to Chester, where Mr. Knight took charge of a flour mill. They were congratulated by their friends for getting off from the river and going to the interior, where they would be comparatively safe from the contagion. Human foresight was a failure. In Chester they took a house situated on the lot where the postoffice stands at present. On the west end of the lot was a small brick schoolhouse, used also for religious or church assemblies. The first case of cholera was Dr. James S. Hibbard, who had been called to Syracuse to prescribe for a man who was sick, a steamboat man just returned from a trip on the river. Dr. Hibbard pronounced the case cholera and prescribed accordingly. On his way back to Chester he was attacked with the malady and, getting off from his horse, took a dose of calomel, lay down by the roadside and fell asleep in the woods. As soon as he was able to remount his horse he proceeded homeward. He finally recovered. This occurred in July. Soon afterwards a son of Jasper Branch, about fourteen years of age, came to his work in the mill from his dinner, was taken violently ill and was assisted to an upper room, but grew rapidly worse, and before nightfall he was dead. That night a sister, older than he, took sick and died before morning. Two deaths in Mr.

Branch's family was a shock to the community. Two or three weeks elapsed, and then a show came to Tupper's Plains, which Lewis Nye, a youth, attended and remained over night. He was stricken with the cholera next morning and died in a few hours. Next in order of time was the family of John Ware, a saddler. He had a large family, but the father, mother and four children fell victims to the cholera. First the daughter Polly, a young woman, returned from church in the evening, apparently well, but that night she died. The next day two of her brothers were snatched away, and the second day the father and mother joined the dead children. Relatives of the Ware family came up from Gallipolis to help care for them, and took the survivors home, one boy dying on the way. Five children remained, who lived, married and settled in Meigs county, Gallia and Mason, W. Va. William Ware never married; lived in his sister's home and died there at Miller McGlothlin's, near Ravenswood, W. Va.

Charles Doane, a tanner, was suddenly attacked after a talk with Dr. Carpenter in a light vein, "that after the people all died, he and the doctor would open a hotel." After parting, in fifteen minutes the message was sent to the doctor of his sickness, and in one hour Charles Doane was dead.

William Torrence was stricken by the epidemic, but rallied for a time, then relapsed and died after an illness of fourteen days. Mr. Harold Wells nursed William Torrence fourteen nights in succession without taking off his clothes to go to bed. Later, Myron Wells, Baza Wells, their mother and a sister were each prostrated with the disease, while Harold, the brother and son, attended them, and they all recovered.

A son of Marcus Bosworth, about ten years of age, went to bed as usual, but later called his mother, "so very sick," and, although medicine was administered at once, by 10 o'clock the child was dead. A Mr. Horton, aged about forty-five years, was one of the fatal victims. Harold Wells, Otis Hardy and Van Weldon were busy all the time ministering to the sick and burying the dead. Mr. Weldon was a cabinet maker and made the coffins for those who died. This history of the cholera in 1834 in Chester we believe correct and authentic. S. C. L.

An incident occurred in 1833 in Lebanon township, below Sandy, when the cholera was epidemic in New Orleans and many cities, that a steamboat landed on the Ohio side of the river near a small graveyard on the bank and sent a messenger to a house not far away for permission to bury a man, then dead on the boat. The request was denied with rudeness, so frightened was the householder at the approach of cholera. The man was buried by the roadside. No case of the disease appeared in the neighborhood until the next summer, when the man who refused the stranger a grave was stricken with cholera and died, the only death from cholera ever known in the place.

The second visitation of cholera at Middleport, in 1849, resulted in the deaths of four persons in the Baily family—Mr. David Baily and his wife, his daughter and son-in-law; also Mrs. Hudson, a sister of Mr. Bailey. Oren Jones was their nurse. He was a young man and claimed that by his strong will he was able to resist the contagion. There were a few cases of cholera in Pomeroy in 1849, but we are not in possession of details. In the first seasons of the epidemic there were fatalities of some persons about Letart. Balser Roush and family, living above Racine, in Letart township, were victims; several of them died. Dr. J. B. Ackley gave medical attention and secured assistance for care of such as needed.

Job Story, of Bedford township, was one of the early settlers of that township and a pioneer abolitionist, who ever dared to vote his sentiments even in old Bedford. He died March 18th, 1883, aged ninety-one years.

Frederic Merrill and Arthur Merrill were brothers, who were born in Newburyport, Mass., and moved with their father to Cincinnati in 1823. The family came to Meigs county in 1830. Frederic Merrill was a merchant in Rutland village. He was a township trustee several years, but returned to Cincinnati, where he died in 1844.

Arthur Merrill graduated in a law school and came to Rutland in 1834. He served as probate judge in Meigs county six years. Died in Rutland April 18th, 1881, aged sixty-eight years.

Samuel Pomeroy owned the valuable coal lands first developed in and near the town of Pomeroy, at the first quarter of the nineteenth century. Much territory of the Ohio Company's Purchase is seen on the records of Gallia county and of Washington county as entered by Abigail Dabney, and later was transferred to other parties, Mr. Samuel Pomeroy, a relative, a Boston man, who lived in Cincinnati in 1833, at the time that his daughter, Clara Alsop Pomeroy, became the wife of Valentine B. Horton, a young lawyer from Pittsburgh, Pa. Mr. Horton was born January 29th, 1802, in Windsor, Vt., having taken a military training and also a regular course in law, and after his marriage came directly to Pomeroy, Ohio, in 1833, where he opened up the coal industry that gave Meigs county its greatest commercial importance and laid out the town of Pomeroy.

Mr. Samuel Pomeroy built a fine residence just back of the present Court House, but died soon afterwards. The history of V. B. Horton cannot receive adequate notice in these brief articles, and belongs in fact to a later time than the real pioneer period of the early settlers. Mr. Horton died in Pomeroy, January 13th, 1888, at the age of 86 years.

Mrs. Clara Alsop Horton was born in Boston, October 7th, 1804, and with her husband made their home in Pomeroy during fifty-four years of their wedded life. Her courteous manners and fine intellectual equipment made her the peer of any lady in any land. Her gracious charity and broad views of life gave her influence with the best class of people in social, civil or religious life. She was a devout Episcopalian, and her husband built and donated to the town of Pomeroy the elegant stone church of that denomination. She was a wise, exemplary wife and mother. They had a family of five children: Clara Pomeroy Horton became the wife of Gen. John Pope. Francis Dabney Horton was married to Gen. M. F. Force of Cincinnati. Edwin Johnson Horton married a daughter of Dr. Estes Howe of Boston. Annie Alsop Horton died in childhood.

Samuel Dana Horton became noted as a writer of prominence in monetary affairs, lived on the Continent of Europe, and married a daughter of a retired British officer in Switzerland.

Catharine Alsop Horton was the wife of John May of Boston.

Mrs. Clara A. Horton died September 28th, 1894, nearly ninety years of age, at the home of her daughter, Mrs. Force, in Sandusky, Ohio.

Martin Heckard, a lawyer, came to Meigs county about 1838 or 1839, not certain as to date. He located in Pomeroy and married Miss Catharine P. Horton, a sister of the Hon. V. B. Horton. Mr. Heckard was the first Probate Judge of Meigs county; and served three years. They had a family of three children. George Heckard, Lucy Heckard died in young womanhood. Mary Heckard went to school on the Hudson, and became the wife of Mr. Huntington of Long Island. Judge Heckard died in Pomeroy. Mrs. Heckard died at her daughter's, Mrs. Huntington, January 9th, 1890, aged seventy-nine years.

Jacob Rice, born at Murrayville, Pa., January 2nd, 1790. He married Hannah Plummer, who died leaving one child, Henry Rice of Rutland. Mr. Jacob Rice died November 3d, 1888, aged 98 years, 10 months, 1 day, in Salisbury township.

Ira McCumber was born July 5th, 1805, in Gallia county, and married Mary Boyer, who was born April 29th, 1807, in Pennsylvania. They lived in Salem township, and Mr. McCumber died April 14th, 1882, aged 77 years.

Mrs. McCumber died May 5th, 1895, aged 88 years. She was a member of the Pioneer Association, and died in Salem.

The fugitive slave law was brought to notice by two men who had captured a slave belonging to one of the party, and had taken him before a justice of the peace in Gallia county, O. They requested a trial, and certificate for the removal of the slave from the State. The justice appointed the trial to be made the next day at 10 o'clock a. m. An anti-slavery man who learned when the suit was to held, started at once to Rutland for Nathan Simpson, a lawyer of local fame. The following morning Mr. Simpson and his friend started for that magistrate's office to watch proceedings. What could be done? Evidently the master had all the proof that the law required. When the lawyer's party got within a few miles of the place, they began announcing their mission and inviting people, every man they saw or could send word to, "to come and see the fun."

At the hour, 10 o'clock, Mr. Simpson went into the courtroom and talked with the owner; also with the slave, and offered to see that he had a fair trial. At first, he opened the case very mildly, but as the house filled up, the crowd looking through the doors and windows and every place where they could see or hear, Simpson's voice became louder and increased in pathos and energy with little thought about correctness of language or logic. The slave owner became alarmed, fearing the mob had collected to lynch him, and with his party slipped out of a back door, saying, "He would never follow another slave into Ohio, for when they get there they are beyond our reach." It is claimed that this case was the last capture of a slave in Ohio. 1850.

James Petty was born in old Virginia in 1819, and came when quite young with his parents to Pagetown, Meigs county. His father Hugh Petty moved to Gallia county subsequently, and died there. James Petty married in that county, but lost his wife soon afterwards, when with his widowed mother, he came to Rutland, and remained there the rest of his life. He held many responsible local offices, justice of the peace, for many years. He made a home for his aged mother and invalid sister with filial and brotherly devotion. His death occurred in Rutland, Ohio, January 26th, 1891, aged seventy-two years.

Mrs. A. Hoff—neé More—was born in Parkersburg, W. Va., on November 1st, 1819, and was married to J. D. Hoff January 29th, 1839. They came to Letart, Ohio, in 1845, and to Middleport, Ohio, in 1849. She united with the Methodist Episcopal Church in her fourteenth year, and lived a consistent and useful life. She died in Middleport, July 18th, 1883.

Lucinda H. Dunham, wife of Hiram B. Smith, was born in Washington county, Ohio, November 20th, 1808. She was the daughter of Amos Dunham and wife—neé Laura M. Guthrie, from whom she inherited a liberal share of physical and mental qualities. She obtained a fair English education at Marietta, Ohio. The family came to Pomeroy in 1837, where she became the wife of Mr. H. B. Smith, a lawyer and prominent man in business and social circles in Pomeroy, Ohio. He was an active member and president of the Miegs County Pioneer Association for several years. They had one son, who died in early manhood. Mrs. Smith died in Pomeroy, Ohio, March 17th, 1881.

Catharine Dawson was born July 17th, 1820, in Beaver county, Pa., and was married to Dr. Joseph Dickson, October 19th, 1841. They moved to Athens county the same year. They had five children, three of whom died in childhood. Dr. Dickson went with a company overland to California in 1849, and was killed by the accidental discharge of his own revolver soon after reaching California. December 11th, 1864, Mrs. Dickson was married to Mr. Josiah Simpson, of Rutland, Ohio, and removed to his home with her two daughters. She died June 4th, 1895. She had been a faithful member of the Free Will Baptist Church, a most excellent woman.

The Bradbury family. Contributed by Judge Samuel Bradbury in 1895, to the Meigs County Pioneer Association.

"Seventy-nine years ago, December, 1816, the parents of Judge Samuel Bradbury floated down the Ohio river in a little boat and tied up at the mouth of Leading creek, where they entered a small log cabin, and with their seven children became citizens of the great State of Ohio. The father had but one dollar and fifty cents in his pocket when he landed. The family came from Maine, having made their way through the wilderness as best they could. Samuel was seven years old at that time. One son was born after the arrival in Ohio, who died at the age of thirty-eight years. The family were reared to honorable lives, and the sons achieved merited distinction in positions of honor and trust. The seven children lived to an average age of eighty-three years."

Judge Samuel Bradbury was born in Maine, August 4th, 1809, and died in Middleport, Ohio, March 1st, 1897, aged eighty-seven and one-half years. He had been one of the most active and efficient men in the organization of the Meigs County Pioneer Association in 1876.

Simeon Elliott was a brother of Judge Fuller Elliott, and came to Meigs, rather Washington county, in 1797, and bought land, situated back from the Ohio river, in what was later included in Sutton township. He married Lucy Putnam, a distant relative of George W. Putnam. They had a large family, reared to honorable positions in the community, in a home of refinement not common in those days. The sons were: Rev. Madison Elliott, a graduate of Marietta College and of Lane Seminary, Cincinnati, Ohio. He was the principal of the academy at Chester in 1844-45, a flourishing institution at that time. Miss Clarissa Cutler, a daughter of Hon. Ephraim Cutler, was the vice-principal. Two other sons were Putnam Elliott, who died in early manhood, and Sumner Elliott, who emigrated to some Western state years ago. The daughters were: Nancy Elliott, Maria, Mrs. William Torrence; he died of cholera; then she married Mr. Phineas Robinson. Lucy, Mrs. Josiah Branch; Lury Ann, Mrs. Orin Branch; Adaline, Mrs. Elihu Stedman; Fidelia, and Lydia died unmarried.

Mr. Simeon Elliott was called "Squire" Elliott, in distinction from Judge Fuller Elliott, M. D. He built a tread mill run by horse-power, and attached to the machinery a carding machine. Mrs. Elliott, after being a widow many years, married Abel Chase, Sr., of Rutland.

Samuel Branch settled in Chester township in 1807. He married Miss Tryphena Stedman, a sister of Levi Stedman, so long prominent in public affairs.

Mr. Branch was a Free Will Baptist preacher, and opened his own house for preaching; also built a schoolhouse on his own land for the education of the children of the neighborhood. Mr. Branch was ready to assist in any enterprise for the benefit in morals or education in the community. They had a large family of sons and daughters.

Samuel Branch, Jr., was a Baptist preacher. Harry and William were farmers. Josiah Branch married Lucy Elliott, and kept a store in Chester. Orin Branch married Lury Ann Elliott; they had one daughter, Julia. Mrs. Lury Ann Branch died early. Orin Branch moved to Pomeroy, and was county treasurer several years. His second wife was Miss Josephine Paige, an excellent woman. Hosmer Branch married and settled in Pomeroy, engaged in mercantile business. They had several children.

Mary Branch was married three times—Wallace and Spicer were two of them. Lucy Branch was the wife of James Madison Cooper. Miranda Branch was married to Mr. Cline; lived in Pagetown. Rev. Samuel Branch, Sr., was a pioneer of the type to be honored and remembered.

Some old, yellow papers, found among the Levi Stedman's documents, have been furnished for notice in the Revised Pioneer History of Meigs County by Miss Eva L. Walker, of Chester, Ohio, as belonging to the estate of Mr. Levi Stedman, her great-grandfather, and we take pleasure in copying several of them, while all of them are interesting specimens of the writing and transactions of the pioneer period. We copy first a parchment deed, a land warrant, signed by James Monroe, President, with official seal of the United States of America attached.

I, James Monroe, President of the United States of America, to all to whom these presents shall come, greeting:

Know ye, that in pursuance of the acts of Congress, appropriating and granting land to the late army of the United States, passed on and since the sixth of May, 1812, Dinah Byram, only heir at law of Adam Ball, having deposited in the General Land Office a warrant in her favor, numbered 24689, there is granted unto the said Dinah Byram, only heir at law of Adam Ball, late a private in Holt's Company of the Seventeenth Regiment of Infantry, a certain tract of land containing one hundred and sixty acres, being the northwest quarter of Section 6, of Township 1 south, Range 5 east, in the tract appropriated (by the act aforesaid) for military bounties, in the territory of Arkansas, to have and to hold, the said quarter section of land, with the appurtenances thereof, unto the said Dinah Byram, only heir at law of Adam Ball, December 9th, and to her heirs and assigns forever.

In testimony whereof, I have caused these letters to be made patent, and the seal of the General Land Office to be hereunto affixed. Given under my hand, at the City of Washington, this sixteenth day of July, in the year of our Lord one thousand, eight hundred and twenty-one, and of the independence of the United States of America the forty-sixth.

{ Seal of the General Land Office U. S. A. } By the President,

JAMES MONROE.

JOSIAH MEIGS,

Commissioner of General Land Office. Exd.

Recorded, Vol. 6, 7255. · J. Wheaton.

Levi Stedman, Esq., to Matthew Buell, Dr.:

1811.		
May 9th.	To 8 doses of physic, et gm. opie........	$3 00
1812.		
Aug. 10th.	" Jal. Senna	25
Sept. 12th.	" Gm. Opie et Rad. Dianthus..........	1 50
1813.		
April 2nd.	Sundry Articles, Medicine, Advice and attend'e	12 50
May 4th.	Elix. Vit. I. loz. Cham. Emetic, I art., &c.	2 50
July 1st.	Visits to Daughter, Sundry Art. Medicine.	15 00
		36 25
Aug. 18th.	Puley Ipecac Rheumatic Liniment, Elix. p— (non-readable) Ex. Jr., Wife............	2 50
		$38 75

Dolls. 130. —— cts. No. 131.

General Post Office.
Washington City, July 1st, 1819.

Sir—At sight, pay to Skinner & Barber, or order, One hundred and thirty dollars, and charge to account of this Office.

ABRAM BRADBURY,
Assistant Post-Master General.

To Levi Stedman, Esq.
Post Master, at Stedman's Mills,
Chester, O.

Aug. 29, 1820.

Order from M. Segrist, to Mr. Levi Stedman, Shade river, Ohio.

Let Thomas Haywalt have three galls. of Whiskey, in exchange for Rye, to be delivered at the Ferry, and oblige, Yours Resp'y,

MICHAEL SEGRIST.

Mason, Va.

The deed of the land from Dinah Byram to Dorothy Stedman and Joel Cowdery, executors of the will of Levi Stedman, deceased, executed and acknowledged before Randall Stivers, justice of the peace, signed Dinah + Byram (Her mark), and recorded by Recorder of Meigs county, 1824. David Barber, Clerk.

Receipts of money for different purposes.

A deed of ten acres of land from Josiah Vining to Dorothy Stedman to satisfy a judgment for eighteen dollars and sixty cents, with the costs accruing thereto.

Recorded in Volume 2nd, page 80 and 81. Chas. Gardiner, Recorder.

Gallia County.

Gallipolis, December 31st, 1805.

Received of Levi Stedman, Collector of taxes for Letart Township, the sum of Thirty Dollars and thirty-two cents ½, on account of the County tax of this township, for the year 1805.

FRANCIES LE CLERQ, Ex (torn out).

Received of Levi Stedman $4.20 cts. for his tax on 420 acres of land — 12, Range 3, T. 24 S. Athens Co. for 1819.

ISAAC BARKER, Coll'r.

The Pilchard and Ellis families came from the eastern shore of Maryland to Ohio, about the year 1810, and settled in Letart, Ohio. Peter Pilchard's wife was a Miss Roloff. They had several children, Lewis, Lybrand and others. Lewis Pilchard married Esther Hayman, a daughter of Josiah Hayman, and located in Letart Falls, W. Va. Lybrand Pilchard married and made his home in East Letart, and brought up a family. He was a member of the Methodist Episcopal Church, an active, loyal adherent to its usages, serving as steward, class leader or Sunday school superintendent, and brought up a highly respectable family.

John Ellis, Sr., lived in Letart many years. He had two sons, John R. Ellis and Henry Ellis. John R. Ellis married Elizabeth Ford, and had a family of sons and daughters. Milton Ellis served in the war for the Union, and was promoted to the rank of major. William A. Ellis was a soldier, also, in the cavalry service, and won distinction for courage. Esther Ellis was married to Hiram L. Sibley, a soldier in the army, but was held a prisoner in the Libby prison, Richmond, Va., for several months. After the close of the war he opened a law office in Marietta, Ohio, and became distinguished for his legal talents. He served as circuit judge in this district, and as a delegate to the General Conference of the Methodist Episcopal Church, in each capacity repeatedly.

Regina Ellis remained ministering to the needs of her parents in their last years with filial devotion. John R. Ellis was elected as a county commissioner several terms, and was a Sunday school superintendent for more than forty years. Mrs. Elizabeth Ellis died in her ninety-eighth year.

Henry Ellis married Adaline Johnson, daughter of an old resident of Chester township. They lived in Racine, Ohio; had two children, Jeremiah A. Ellis, who married and moved to Kansas. Mary E. Ellis was married to Dorr DeWolf, one of a family of steamboat men. Their home has been in Racine. Mrs. Mary E. DeWolf is a loyal Methodist.

Mr. Henry Ellis died in middle life, and Mrs. Adaline Ellis did not attain old age. They were good citizens, highly esteemed by the community.

In the earlier days, the schoolboy's equipment was scant, made up chiefly by the mother's ingenuity, in co-operation with the father's desire to give some "book learning" to his children. Money was hard to obtain, and the necessities of life were secured by traffic. For writing purposes, an ink was made by an infusion of oak gall nuts, mixed with beef's gall and vinegar, in proportions learned by experiments. Another kind of ink in use was made from a decoction of maple bark, carefully poured off, and a lump of copperas and a little sugar added to the liquid. The sugar gave a gloss to the writing, and this ink was a good black, but if too much sugar was put in, the written pages would stick together.

For schools and ordinary purposes, a thick, unruled paper, called foolscap, was in use, and the ruling was made with lead pencils cut off in strips from the lead of which bullets were made, and hammered into shape, flat and narrow, about three inches in length. These lead pencils were drawn across the paper by a straight-edged ferule. Pens were made from quills taken from the wings of geese. The schoolmaster called the children into school by rapping loudly on the door—never had a bell. The sessions were from 8 or 9 o'clock a. m. to 4 or 5 o'clock in the afternoon, six days in the week for a three months' term in winter. Some teachers had a watch, but, if lacking that, a good look at the sun was a common way of reckoning time. E. L. B.

April 12th, 1819, the first Court of Common Pleas for Meigs county, on petition of Thomas Ridding, of Sutton, for a license to keep a house of entertainment in his dwelling house, it was ordered that license be given him on his complying with the requisitions of the law. Thomas Ridding had a license, previously granted, to keep a ferry at Graham's Station, Meigs county, Ohio.

The hotel, as described by Mr. Ridding's daughter, "was a double log cabin—two log houses with a space of ten feet between them, but all included under one roof—and having a spacious attic for common sleeping rooms. The patrons of this hostelry were men who carried on trade up and down the Ohio river in pirogues, or large canoes, laden with flour, salt and groceries, for sale to the people on shore, and who did a good business in exchanging commodities for skins, furs and ginseng. These boatmen would make their stopping place at night at the Ridding house at Graham's Station. Sometimes two or three boat crews would land at the same time. They were sure of a bountiful meal of substantial food, and when the beds were all filled, if necessary the landlady would make field beds on the floor. There was no grumbling at the lack of washbowl and pitcher, nor any scrambling for a looking-glass. They were glad to sleep after the hard day of poling canoes. This tavern had a sad closing up. Mr. Ridding was accidentally drowned, and his widow went back to her old home in the Shenandoah valley. Narrative by Mrs. Cynthia Philson, Racine, Ohio.

The first newspaper published in Meigs county was dated November 1st, 1843, called "The Weekly Times," edited and printed by L. Beatty. In a year or two the paper was edited by O. B. Chapman, with Mr. Beatty. In 1845 and 1846, R. T. Van Horn was associated with Mr. Chapman, and the name was changed to "The Meigs County Telegraph." Later, Mr. Van Horn withdrew, and the paper was under the management of T. A. Plants, Esq. The paper had a change of names and editors until 1860—O. B. Chapman editor and E. S. Trussell business manager. Mr. Chapman was a good editor and practical printer, and no slovenly typesetting was ever seen while he was editor. He held the place longer than any one before or afterwards. Mr. E. S. Trussell succeeded Mr. Chapman, and continued to publish a good, influential paper. Mr. O. B. Chapman finally, after many vicissitudes in fortune, died in Colorado Springs, at the advanced age of eighty years, a true, noble-hearted man, steadfast in his principles of righteousness in civil or religious matters.

The next paper was "The People's Fountain," a temperance paper, printed by Hoy and Rundle, in 1854. It failed after a few years for lack of patronage. The first paper printed in Middleport was "The Meigs County News," in 1871, by E. S. Branch. S. C. L.

"The Buckeye Rovers."—An article in the Cincinnati Enquirer by Arthur B. Harding, and copied into this manuscript by S. C. Larkin:

"The Buckeye Rovers crossed the continent to the California gold fields in 1849. There were twenty-two men in the party, from Athens and Meigs counties exclusively. From Athens county: Elza Armstrong, W. S. Stedman, Hugh Dickson, Dennis Drake, Elijah Terrill, Solomon Townsend, James Shepherd, William Logan, W. T. Wilson, Joseph Dickson, M. D., R. P. Barnes, John Banks, George Reeves, Asa Condee, M. D., H. L. Graham. From Meigs county: Seth Paine, L. D.

Stevens, J. C. Rathburn, M. D., Joshua Gardner, Charles Giles, John S. Giles. Fifteen Athenians and seven Meigs countians.

The party left Albany April 9th, 1849, and, going to Middleport, Meigs county, embarked on a steamboat and, further on, by boats until reaching Lexington, Mo. Here they organized, choosing Dr. Joseph Dickson captain. Cattle were brought that never had seen a yoke, and a week was spent in breaking them. The party drove one hundred miles to St. Joseph, where, if they had waited to cross the ferry in their turn, they would have been delayed six weeks, so great was the rush westward. Luckily, some of them were old river men, and who constructed a rude craft, that carried them over the river in four days. They proceeded up the Platte river by Fort Kearney and Fort Laramie, and to the north of the Great Salt Lake, eighty miles. Cholera infested the plains at this time, and for more than a thousand miles west of Fort Kearney, if there had been no trail, they could easily have kept their course by the new made graves. They had many thrilling experiences and narrow escapes from the Indians. At the sink of the Humboldt river the Indians stole all of their cattle. Then the company disbanded, and each one had to get to Sacramento the best way he could. Judge Wilson fell in with an Illinois party going to Oregon, and he was the first white man at Downieville, on the Yuba river, where he subsequently took up the largest nugget any of them secured. It was about the size of a goose egg and was valued at $1285. On September 20th, 1849, the first of the Buckeye Rovers reached Sacramento, then consisting of only one wooden structure and used for a postoffice. The tent population was about 5000, which increased as by magic, so that in less than one year it was estimated at 80,000 souls. When they reached the golden land, labor was worth $16 a day, but dropped to $10 the next season. Provisions of all kinds were brought from the Sacramento valley on mules and sold at enormous prices. Everything sold by the pound, at $1, except butter, which was $4.

Once they paid $8 for a pound of soda to make slapjacks. Letters from the East cost 40 cents postage, and were usually a year in reaching their destination. A man at the diggings was employed as mail carrier. He took a list of the names of the miners and went to San Francisco, the nearest postoffice, 200 miles distant. On reaching the office, he had to hunt the letters that were wanted from a large pile on the floor. They paid the mail carrier $2 for each letter carried or received. In the winter of '49 Condee and Wilson formed a partnership with two Illinois men, Burroughs and Barnes by name, for the purpose of prospecting on the Yuba river. There were no towns and no laws, but among themselves. They agreed that each miner was to have thirty feet on the river as his claim. After staking out four claims near Downieville, Barnes and Burroughs went farther up the mountains prospecting, leaving the others to guard the claims. The miners began to swarm in, and it was useless to try to hold the claims. "The upper two we thought were good," said Judge Wilson, "but the lower two we sold to a party of Georgians for $1000, and shortly afterwards I saw them take out between $40,000 and $50,000 worth of gold dust. My share in the upper claim I sold in a few weeks later for $2300." It was a common occurrence for a miner to be worth $1000 one day and be as much in debt the next day from losses in gambling. There was not much stealing in the mining region, for among the miners, if a person was caught stealing anything to the amount of $1 or more the penalty was a severe whipping or death.

The first of the Rovers that died was Dr. Joseph Dickson, who was accidentally shot by dropping his revolver while prospecting on the American river. Mr. Stedman spent eleven years in California.

Judge Wilson served four years in the Civil War, and he says "the hardships endured were trifling in comparison with the overland trip to California in 1849." A few of the men who went out with this expedition returned home with financial gains, but the majority were not so fortunate.

The Associate Judges of Meigs County, Ohio.

Date of Election.	Names of Judges.	Terms.
February 6th, 1819..	Fuller Elliott, M. D.	2 years
January 17th, 1821..	George Burns	2 years
January 23d, 1823..	Peter Grow	4 years
January, 1827......	Henry L. Osborn, appointed to fill one year for Grow	1 year
January 25th, 1828..	Nial Nye	7 years
January 25th, 1835..	Henry L. Osborn	7 years
February 17th, 1842.	William Ledlie	7 years
March 17th, 1849...	William McAboy	3 years
	Total	33 years
February 6th, 1819..	Orasho (Horatio) Strong	5 years
January, 1824......	Cushing Shaw	7 years
January 22d, 1831...	Eli Sigler	7 years
February 10th, 1838.	Nathan Simpson	6 years
February 28th, 1844.	Samuel Bradbury	7 years
February 17th, 1851.	Samuel Bradbury	1 year
	Total	33 years
February 6th, 1819..	James E. Phelps	3 years
In 1822...........	Abel Larkin, appointed to fill one year for J. E. Phelps	1 year
January 23d, 1823..	Abel Larkin	7 years
February 22d, 1830.	John C. Bestow	7 years
February 16th, 1837.	John C. Bestow	7 years
1844, 1851.........	Henry L. Osborn	7 years
	Total	33 years

Lists furnished by Mr. Charles Matthews, Washington, D. C.:

Names of all persons in 1820 in Salisbury township, from Census Report.—Joseph Bradford, David Bradford, Charles Wright, William T. Whitney, David Lindsey, Joel Smith, Benjamin Smith, Frederic Frazier, Josiah Vining, Paris Eccleston, Perry Hardin, Alvin Rathburn, Sarah Bullock, Benjamin Williams, David Osork, Daniel Rathburn, Cyrus Higley, Archibald Murray, George Russell, Daniel McNaughton, Joel Higley, John Winkley, Samuel Risley, Samuel L. Wilder, Charles Jones, Frederic Hysell, Isaac Meeker, Timothy Smith, Erastus Saus, Robert B. Harris, Isa Russell, Joseph Vining, Increase Jones, James Smith, Edward Hysell, Caleb Austin, William Kerr, John Woodward, Strother Hysell, John Smith.

Names of all persons living in Rutland township and Salisbury township in 1820.—George Russell, Benson Jones, Abel Larkin, Silas Clark, James McGuire, William Hobart, Joshua Parker, Ebenezer Howard, Samuel Vining, John Knight, Cornelius Bradshaw, Amos Partlow, John Baily, Jeptha Mason, Benjamin Frost, David Bailey, Samuel Gilman, Isaac Hugg, Samuel Gilman, Jr., Elias Grigsby, Joseph Saxton, Eli Wright, Robert Hysell, Samuel Lyman, Richard Vining, John Lynas, Elam Higley, Daniel Rathburn, Jr., Alvin Bingham, James E. Phelps, Philip Jones, Samuel Everett, Hamilton Kerr, Benjamin T. Clough, William Dodson, William Baily, John Kindall, George Knapp, Nathanael Bean, Lariah Norris, Isaac Smith, Jans Bingham, Silas Knight, John Hysell, Brewster Higley.

Salem township, 1820.—William Parker, Peter Aleshire, John S. Giles, Cushing Shaw, Ozias Strong, Jacob Swett, John Williams, Jame McClure, William Green, L. V. Vonschritz, John Fordice, Eleazer Crowell, Mark Malone, Chauncey Knowlton, Sampson Nelson.

CYCLONE IN COLUMBIA TOWNSHIP IN MAY, 1886.

[Condensed from a report in the Telegraph.]

May 12th, at 11 o'clock p. m. two dark clouds were seen approaching each other from opposite points of the north and of the south. They met, and the roar of the concussion was terrific. The clouds commingled and seemed to fall to the earth, moving with electric speed and resistless fury. The first house struck was a log building occupied by J. Q. Adams and his family of seven persons. The house was demolished, but the inmates escaped injury. Next in the course of the storm were the barn and sheep houses of Mr. Gregory; then a school house; on, tearing off the upper story of the dwelling of E. Foster; then more barns, until it narrowed down to a track of not more than 300 yards in width, keeping near the ground. A new house of Nathan Vail was badly shaken; another house torn down. The upper story of T. D. Jackson's house, with a large stone chimney, was tumbled over the inmates in bed; one person injured; his barn blown to pieces; two horses and eighteen sheep were killed. The home of S. D. Wilcox was wrecked, and the furious storm went on, flattening shrubbery, sweeping away fences, twisting oak trees like wisps around each other. Then it reached the house of Mrs. McComas, who, with her granddaughter of ten years, was sleeping in one room, while in another room was a grandson twenty years old. Everything was swept from its place; the house, granaries, all were wrecked. The married son, who lived near, ran to the place as soon as possible; first found the little girl, apparently lifeless, but who was resuscitated. The old lady was found fifty yards to the south, stripped of clothing and dead. The young man lay in another direction, with broken neck and legs.

Many sheep were killed. A fine orchard of J. L. Carpenter was prostrated. The depot of the K. & M. Railroad was cut in two, dividing it from the roof to the ground, and carried eastward. A frame dwelling of Mr. McKnight was torn away. The father, mother and daughter, having heard the storm coming, threw themselves flat on the floor, face downwards, and the house was borne away from over their heads, the wind catching them up and pitching them with great force on the ground. Mrs. McKnight had two ribs broken, and Mr. McKnight was badly bruised, but they succeeded with great difficulty in reaching the house of Dr. Dudgeon, a neighbor who, fortunately, had escaped the hurricane. A cloudburst of rain followed immediately, that prevented conflagration, as the air was charged with electricity. Mr. Jewell's blacksmith shop was cleared of all its fixtures. In leaving the ground, the wind retained its strength, for a lot of standing timber had the tops cut off at an angle of thirty degrees from the base until "out of the woods." The storm lasted about two hours, but the havoc was the work of a few minutes. A memorable event for Columbia township.

In 1817 four young men from Kentucky, evidently of wealthy parentage, well dressed, with nice boots, traveling on foot to see the country in Ohio, being weary and footsore, stopped a few days at Judge Larkin's to recuperate. One day, near sunset, the judge came in from his work to have a little talk. They said to him: "You have no slaves in Ohio. We should think it very wearisome to do all your own work. And then it deprives you of an opportunity to acquire knowledge. We have slaves to do our work. Then we can go to town, or any place to talk, and hear all the news, and so acquire information." They were told "that those who had the best chance did not always get the most knowledge." One of the number, in order to change the subject, asked Judge Larkin, "Where did you come from?" He replied, "From New England." They said, "New England must be a big state, we find so many that come from that state." They were informed New England was not a state, but was composed of five states. "Did you never hear of the State of Massachusetts, New Hampshire, Vermont or Connecticut?" They were hard to convince, but finally said they thought they were towns or counties.

Soon after the organization of the county of Meigs a company of prominent citizens of Athens purchased lands of the Ohio Company's Purchase, situated as river bottom farms, above Old Town creek, and farther above the Hall property on the Ohio river border. The lands were heavily timbered. Mr. Ziba Lindley, Sr., Ziba Lindley, Jr., Elmus Lindley, Col. Charles Shipman and Nehemiah Bicknell, who had his home with the Shipman family. Col. Shipman built a two-story hewed-log house, well finished, in which he had a storeroom for general merchandise. Mr. Ziba Lindley, Sr., put up a house of logs, hewn on the inner side, with floors, doors, windows and partitions done by a regular "house joiner." Ziba Lindley, Jr., erected a two-story hewed-log house, well finished as to floors, doors, windows and bedroom partitions, a stone chimney, with open fireplaces to each story. Elmus Lindley had the farm adjoining his brother Ziba's and built a smaller house. Mr. Bicknell bought his farm later, where he built a hewed-log house, one and a half stories high, with inner house-joiner finishings and stone chimney. The lumber for all of these buildings was brought from Wright's mill on Mill creek, Virginia. There was an old cabin on the back part of the Shipman farm that was taken for a schoolhouse, and Miss Harriet Bartlett taught school there in the summer. Colonel Shipman conducted religious services there, reading the Scriptures and a sermon on Sundays, and on Sunday afternoons sometimes they met to sing. There were good singers in the Athens company, and when they met with their note books—patent notes—to sing "Easter Anthem" and "carry all the parts" to time as correct as a military drill, it was quite inspiring. But the native population did not assimilate. They preferred the fiddle and such dances as suited their ideas of pleasure.

The Athens people became discouraged. The elder Mrs. Lindley died and was buried in the pioneer graveyard, and the other families gathered up their children and household goods and moved back to Athens, leaving N. Bicknell agent for all of their farms to rent or sell, as he might have opportunity. In the meanwhile he had married Julia Larkin, of Rutland, and had no alternative but to remain and open up his own farm

SAMUEL S. PAINE

NEHEMIAH BICKNELL

for cultivation, doing a vast amount of hard work. He spoke often of his disappointment in the abandonment of the neighborhood by the Lindleys and Shipmans, as he had anticipated their good influences to bring about a better social environment.

The name of George Ackley is on the record of deeds for land purchased by him in 1800, in a part of Washington county, afterwards included in Meigs county, thus giving the name of a pioneer family. Jeremiah B. Ackley came to Letart about 1831, a young doctor. He had spent some time at the Ohio University at Athens, O., and had prosecuted his studies there as a physician. He located his office at Letart, O., but also practiced medicine in Jackson county, Va. He had an extensive practice on both sides of the river. He married a daughter of Mr. Wright, of Mill Creek, Va., Miss Charlotte Wright, and made their home in Letart.

They had several children, all of whom died in childhood except one son, George K. Ackley, who lived to follow the profession of his father, and was especially noted as a surgeon. He served as army surgeon in the Fourth West Virginia Infantry in the Civil War. Mrs. Charlotte Ackley died in 1838 or 1839.

Dr. J. B. Ackley then entered the arena of politics, and represented Meigs county in the Ohio Legislature, serving one or two terms with fidelity to his constituents and credit to himself. He was a natural orator, and held county audiences in rapt attention while pleading the cause of temperance during the Washingtonian movement. His second wife was Miss Miriam Smith, of Letart. They had one daughter, Kate, a lovely child, who died at the age of six years. Dr. Ackley had moved to Racine, and resumed the practice of medicine, chiefly among the older families. Mrs. Miriam Ackley died in the seventies. In a few years he married Miss Sarah Woods, of Racine, a happy alliance. She lived to make his last years comfortable with faithful care. He passed away, leaving the record of a useful and honorable life.

Dr. John R. Philson came from Maryland in 1839, and settled in Racine, Ohio, where in 1841 he married Miss Cynthia Redding, a daughter of Thomas Redding, who kept the pioneer hotel in Graham Station in 1824. Mrs. Redding married as second husband Jacob Lalance, and their home was made in Sutton township, below Racine, on the river.

Dr. J. R. Philson was associated with Dr. J. B. Ackley for a while, but subsequently opened up a practice as physician independently. He was in a scope of territory the principal doctor, and won distinction for his skill in the treatment of diseases. He was an army surgeon in the Fourth West Virginia, through the war, and while in the service received injuries that resulted in his death. Dr. Philson was elected Senator for the Sixteenth Congressional District of Ohio, and filled the position with fidelity to his constituents and honor to himself. His death was lamented by the community at large, by his many friends, and especially the poor, whom he had treated gratuitously.

He left a widow, two sons and one daughter. The eldest son, Professor Lewis Philson, has been devoted to educational work as teacher and superintendent.

The second son, John Rush Philson, followed his father's profession and has a well-earned popularity as a doctor. A son of Professor Lewis Philson is also a doctor, making three generations in the medical fraternity.

The daughter, Margaret E. Philson, was married to Charles McElroy soon after the Civil War. He was a soldier in some sharp engagements, inducing a loss of vital force that caused an early death.

The elder Mrs. Philson is living, a marvel of clear mind and memory, and Mrs. McElroy is the faithful daughter and Christian woman.

Dr. John McClintock came to Letart, Ohio, from Philadelphia, and opened an office as a regular physician in 1839. He married Nancy Kingree, daughter of Abraham Kingree, of Letart, an old pioneer in 1841.

They had one son, George M. McClintock, who became a prominent and successful business man, but died in his manhood's prime, honored and lamented.

Dr. McClintock made his permanent home on a farm at Apple Grove, and followed his profession continuously for more than forty years, chiefly in Letart township, a wise and skillful doctor. Dr. McClintock was a man of culture and refinement, quiet, yet genial in manner, a good judge of character. He died leaving a widow and son. His life commanded respect, and his name is an honored memory.

REV. ISAAC REYNOLDS.

Isaac Reynolds was born in the State of New York and, with his parents, emigrated to Ohio and settled in Athens county in early days. He was a student in the Ohio University for some time, and while attending school was converted under the preaching of the Rev. John Stewart, a noted minister of the Methodist Episcopal Church. Soon after his conversion he began to preach.

In 1817, Mr. Reynolds traveled Burlington circuit, Rev. Jacob Young, presiding elder. There was an element of evangelistic fervor in his preaching, and among the converts of his ministry was James Gilruth, who became a Methodist preacher of great power and influence, long an active member of the Ohio Conference.

After traveling circuits a few years, he married Miss Maria Williamson, of Washington county, and located. He had a difficulty of the throat that caused him to cease itinerant work.

About 1830 he came to Letart, not certain as to precise date. He taught school and preached occasionally. As a teacher he was popular. He moved to Lebanon township in 1833, and taught the public school several years. After giving up teaching he settled on his farm and opened a small store, and succeeded in establishing a postoffice, called Great Bend, he being appointed postmaster. Mr. Reynolds finally moved to northern California, preaching sometimes until 1876, where he soon "fell on sleep" his work done.

MR. LUCIUS CROSS, SR.

Lucius Cross was born December 30th, 1798, in Mansfield, Connecticut. When he was three years old he was brought to Marietta, Ohio, where he grew up to manhood. He married Thirza Stanley, daughter of Timothy Stanley, a prominent citizen of Washington county, in April, 1822, and came directly to Meigs county, settling on lands back of Racine, in Sutton township. He cleared his land for cultivation, built a tannery on his farm, erected a saw and grist mill on Bowman's run, built flatboats on the river beach at Graham's Station, as it was then called, had his timber all utilized for lumber, cordwood or tanbark. He opened a trade in the South with boats laden with pressed hay and farm products, and by his different industries gave employment to many men. In 1832 he built his large, commodious farm house. Mr. Cross was a real temperance man, and suffered no whisky to be brought to his premises, and his farm house has the record of being the first building erected in Meigs county without whisky or any intoxicating drink. The house was noted for its beauty in construction and situation, considered the best house in the country as a farmer's home. He had some military knowledge and drilled recruits for the army. He left a valuable estate, a widow and nine sons and daughters. He was entirely blind a few years before his death in August, 1883. The sons have been enterprising men, and all of the family married and settled in Racine and vicinity, except the younger son, Edwin

The Alexander Stone House, once the "Mansion House of Letart, Meigs County, Ohio

Cross, who became a physician and followed his profession in Chicago with notable success.

THE ALEXANDERS.

Thomas Alexander, who entered land in Letart township in 1803, died in 1808, aged 80 years. His wife, Elizabeth, died in 1807, aged 77 years. William Alexander, son of Thomas Alexander, lived on the farm purchased by his father, and married Susan Love. They had a family of two sons and three daughters.

Thomas Alexander married Caroline Burns, and their home was on the Alexander farm, where they lived to a great age, having had a family of eleven children, grown up and married. Moses Alexander married Jane Smith, and died early, leaving a wife and four children. His family lived in the Alexander homestead.

The daughters were: Julia, who was married to David O. Hopkins, and whose home was in Racine, Ohio, where she died. They had several children grown to maturity, but parents and children are all dead but one daughter, Mrs. Reese, of Chicago. Mary Alexander was the wife of Albert Woodruff, of Mill Creek. She passed away soon, leaving one daughter. Isabel Alexander was married to Daniel Bibbee, of Letart, and died in a few years, leaving a daughter.

William Alexander, Sr., was one of the first Commissioners in Meigs, and held that office by re-election several terms. He was prominent in local affairs, magistrate, merchant and farmer. He erected the first stone house in Letart, noted in those days for elegance, the "mansion house" of Letart. He died in 1877, and his wife Susan died in 1860.

Dr. David C. Whaley same to Meigs county with his parents in 1832, and has been a resident of Meigs county ever since. He opened the first dentist's office in Pomeroy, and has followed his profession continuously for more than fifty years. Possessed of a fine mind and rare mechanical abilities, he acquainted himself with every scientific method available for the perfecting of his skill in dentistry, for besides the setting of teeth, Dr. Whaley is an artist in studying facial effects, as well as the inserting of molars. He has had also a successful medical practice, limited in extent on account of his proclivities for dental operations.

He married Miss Amy Smith, a daughter of Benjamin Smith, of Middleport, Ohio, who is a direct descendant in the fourth generation from the pioneer James Smith who came to Leading Creek in 1797. They had a family of three children, one son and two daughters. The son, a bright young man, was drowned just as his career was opening as a dentist. The daughters were well educated, and each one has a vocation The elder Miss Whaley is a talented literary woman, and the younger sister is a popular singer in operatic circles, is married and resides in New York City.

THE PAINE FAMILY.

Seth Paine, Sr., came with his family to Ohio from Maine in 1816, and settled in Rutland township. He had four sons, Samuel S. Paine, Bartlett, Seth, Jr., Josiah, and several daughters. The brothers were engaged in the mercantile business in Rutland. Mr. Samuel S. Paine held township offices, as Justice of the Peace, Trustee, and was Postmaster in Rutland. He was elected Recorder of Meigs county when the county seat was removed to Pomeroy, and served in that office for more than twenty years.

He married Miss Martha Cowdery, a daughter of the pioneer Joel Cowdery, who settled on Shade river in 1807. They had two children, a daughter, dying in childhood, and a son, Lewis Paine, who was educated at Kenyon College, Gambier, Ohio. He is a lawyer, has been Probate Judge, and practices his profession in Pomeroy. Mrs. Martha Paine died in 1889, and Mr. Samuel S. Paine died in 1892, both highly esteemed people.

Mr. Bartlett Paine was married twice and had three children, two sons and one daughter. Mr. Seth Paine, 3d, Jr., an expert bookkeeper in Columbus, Ohio, and Dr. Bartlett L. Paine, a noted doctor in Lincoln, Nebraska.

The second wife was Mrs. Aurelia Branch, a widow. Seth Paine, 2d, was one of the "Buckeye Rovers," who went to California in 1849. He was fortunate in business and returned to Rutland a rich man. He married Miss Roxana Rathburn, a daughter of Rev. Elisha Rathburn, a pioneer. The Paine brothers are dead. They were good citizens, enterprising, sterling characters.

Stillman Carter Larkin was born, March 9th, 1808, in Rutland, Ohio, the son of Abel Larkin and Susannah Larkin (neé Bidges), they having moved from Rutland, Vermont, to Ohio in 1804. His childhood, youth, manhood and old age were all spent in Rutland, Ohio. He was a self-educated man, with a philosophical cast of mind, with a clear apprehension of public affairs, and a careful student of political events. A member of the Christian church the greater part of his life, he left the record of a faithful disciple in the performance of religious duties, and the example of an unblemished character. When his father died, his widowed mother chose to remain in the homestead, and this son to take charge of the estate, and to be her protector. This duty he fulfilled with filial tenderness and unremitting care, thus holding the Larkin homestead in his name for a long period of years, and, though married most happily, they had no children. So, when years and infirmities of age were felt, he transferred the "Larkin homestead"—which has now possessed the name for one hundred years—to his nephew, George B. Larkin.

Stillman C. Larkin died January 17th, 1899, aged nearly ninety-one years. Mary Larkin, his widow, died May 30th, 1904, in her ninety-second year of age.

INDEX
TO
PIONEER HISTORY OF MEIGS COUNTY

By STILLMAN CARTER LARKIN